THE BURNING KEY

THE BURNING KEY
New & Selected Poems (1973-2023)

BEATRIX GATES

Thera Books
Sacramento, CA

About the Press

Thera Books is an independent publishing house uplifting the voices of writers across all intersections. Based in Sacramento, California, we aim to publish writers pushing the boundaries of what it means to be human.

for my brother David

and for my beloveds

Contents

New & Reclaimed Poems (2020-2023)

Sunspots
for Rachel Pollack

Evidence a following:
                    sunspots follow each other
                          around the rotating
                              Sun.

Magnetic ropes lie mostly under the surface of the Sun.

    Jumpy fire wings through, loops around and forms pairs of sunspots.

How we shine.

  I can barely remember her name
        Is it her real name?

  We rode together
            perhaps we have the same

             what?   Questions.

If you took an x-ray   could you see that we are
  together at the core
  made from the blood of stars—
  magnetic oppositions— less or more a tangled core.

The radiation grew more intense   hot as hot could be
            spewed a fire ribbon   drove us away
                umbilicus, waving off the edge
      then fusing in two spots like hand-holds for the liquid red plasma.

           We were drawn from deep disturbance—
                 erupting far beyond the surface
             thrashing snaking light
                   flailing arms way way away from us

until memory had to be rediscovered, tooled, located by telescope
             and all the power held.

Can you see iron in the blood of earth, veins:— Is she ours,

       the mother?

What did we do?   It seemed to move through the hands

a fire in the palm like the sounds of a drum:

The sun throbs sounding like a drum every 5 minutes.

Isn't this language enough? Don't you hear me? Where are your hands?

There is blood, a sound, life inside— hot as hot could be...

Disturbance, are you my valentine? Sister in crime?

  Forty years is nothing.   I know your face daring

     lost one.

         I can still see the corona
         around your hair.

Dream for Eva on 7/4 who resists war, always, given 97 years of life, and for Em at 30 who calls out grief and dances a fountain without tears,

1.

Em calls after the slaughter in Colorado Springs—
—I had talk to someone who might have something, I can't even talk. I can't cry.
Have you cried?
—I broke once, a howl. I haven't been able to talk to anyone yet.
My straight friends are talking about it *more*. I'm numb. I can't …
She raises the heat of my heart: Is that hope?
—We will survive these people. They're dead inside. We can't let them kill us.
But they are killing us.
—We have to make it count, whatever it takes to stay alive.
That's how we kill them. Be unafraid of our beauty.
—We came to the same thing. I just can't take it. We have to claim joy!
My Northampton friends, my queer family, we're making a cluster to resist the trauma
    narrative by becoming something else. We're marking our faces with glitter and
    marigolds. To face the world—grief, death and joy! Joy in who we are, every day.
—Remember, playing basketball to squash your feelings and stay hidden. Invisible teen
    star in Maine.
I'm not going back. We answer when we're asked, no matter what. Full of joy and Proud.

2.

In the dream you're celebrating your journey, Eva.
We're moving along a train passageway,
or Grace's hallway in the apartment on W 11th Street. Women's voices,
uncorralled, and men, war resisters all.
We embrace in the passageway,
and you lay down your judgment—
You have a city within you, you are a city—it is within you.
Then, without a landing note, *I feel into things.*
This strikes me as opposite: You have a city within you that I was able to be part of.
We're headed in opposite directions—the train's moving–
you to Europe, to Paris you say to see old friends
and *very old friends* meaning they have passed.
So deeply happy to be on your way,
feeling into the departure.
I study the waking, remaining

city where my life changed and changed again.
I listen for clues.
I must speak to *you* of all people about this time,
the feelings, little time before us, no holding onto it.

Rising over your shoulder, a landscape
of Bread and Puppet creatures on stilts, on sticks
coming up through the trees.

Em called—How are you dealing with this?

      3.

I remember:
it was you, Eva, in white at the Seneca trial
at the Fairgrounds in upstate New York, blistering heat under the tin roof:
it was you who stood as one of many Jane Doe's to protest
for the freedom of assembly and right to passage
down Waterloo's small-town street, blocked by citizens
threatening with flagpoles and one with a gun.
How you sat down quietly with your sisters in nonviolent direct action,
over 50 women arrested on the road together.

I was there on the street,
I was there with women from Maine, a lesbian crew
with our Medusa puppet—wide dark green face,
beautiful copper coiled hair and lavender robe,
large hands: *Freeze the Weapons, Free the World*, Medusa said.
And we were tall, Blue Hill Women for Peace and Justice.
We were seen, we held her high.
Her dark hands swept the air.
I walked under her lavender folds
directing one hand, shaping gesture of welcome
and urgency as she reached her palms out on long sticks.
A man with a flag pole pointed at me, ready to ram us.
A target, her dark hands shadowed the crowd in the midday sun.
When the crowd booed and surged off the sidewalk, we lowered Medusa.
We were in danger carrying her, copper knotted curls locked
and streaming from her skull. Medusa demanded response
and we could not control the response.
We were three women holding her aloft on the road through Waterloo.
By consensus, we decided to leave with Medusa,

take her down and fold the lavender billows around her head, coiled hair,
spread palms and center. We wrapped her tight, couched her under our arms and left.
We wanted to scale the fence guarding the Cruise missiles the next day. We wanted
to be part of the action organized and directed from the women's encampment,
not end torn down, Medusa broken on the street,
become a different kind of weapon.

The March from the Museum at Seneca Falls
to the site of the Cruise missiles dreamed up to honor those
who had come before. The women of the Iroquois nation in the 1590s
who met in Seneca to ask the tribes to cease their war fare.
In 1848, the first Women's Rights Convention convened in Seneca Falls.
And through this same county, where her safe house stands, Harriet Tubman
led slaves north during the 1850s. We wanted to stand with them.
And we were determined to climb over the chain-link fence surrounding the missile
storage site by the Women's Encampment for a Future of Peace and Justice.

4.

And you, Eva, sat down in Waterloo with your Women's Pentagon Action sisters
and War Resister sisters, and Barbara Deming, come from Florida.
You were arrested and taken to a brick school house to be detained,
since the jail was not large enough to hold the number of women
who sat down on the pavement and would not move.
Unstated: fear the jail would be attacked
and damaged, perhaps set on fire. Later, I hear how a local woman and her daughter
came to hear stories from Encampment women who danced and sang
every day outside the jail to comfort their sisters.
The mother/daughter team were quiet,
and said they wanted to hear from the women about why they came to protest.

At the trial at the County Fairgrounds, you spoke about Austria in 1938:
I am a refugee from Vienna, Austria, I am an Austrian who fled the Nazis
as a teenager with my brothers; you spoke about how this blockade
on the bridge reminded you of that time, of the hatred,
and how you would stand firmly, because of that experience
and object with your sisters. You stood against the weapons.

At the site of the trial, a pick up rammed through the Fairgrounds
dragging an effigy of a woman bouncing on the dirt.
Come Bella Abzug who got through to Mario to insist—
we must have protection for these women and this trial at the Fairgrounds.

Cuomo sent state police, a row of police cars with air conditioning,
humming along the rail fence outside the makeshift courthouse at the Fairgrounds.
They stayed in their cars. The presiding judge ordered all the women,
inside and any outside who chanted and interrupted proceedings
to be silent. Women from the encampment sat in small circles in the heat and dust.

Aglow, you testified.
Sweat streaked the sides of your flushed face—
your white tunic and wide pants graceful as you spoke,
walking slowly, gesturing and turning to the judge and the assembled.
Teacher strolling as was your habit, when seeing clearly
your thoughts in the classroom.

The Judge repeated his order for quiet during testimony.
No movement. Spectators were to sit in silence inside or be removed
and any interruption from outside would risk the removal of spectators from the trial.
I sat on bleachers under the broiling tin roof, and I watched you, Eva, in your beautiful
white shirt and pants stand and speak about Austria.

I watched Grace, her graying head and bun pulled back, weave in and out
of the witnessing crowd, holding a baby, daughter of one of those arrested,
and avoid being thrown out of the trial. Witness and decoy,
the baby smiled, happy to be with Grace.
No one touched Grace or the baby as she strolled casually around the tent, peering
outside, then coming back in and walking the aisles, sitting then strolling,
the baby girl at ease on her shoulder.

The judge, a local pharmacist, newly appointed to his seat, listened
for hours on that hot day to the testimony of the Jane Doe's.
He ruled in favor of the women and released them. He said he was moved
by the testimony. They had a right to protest, to assemble, to cross the bridge.
He apologized for the people in the place where he lived.

     5.

This night, on the train—Eva going one way,
I'm going the other. Bright
through the trees: Bread and Puppet beasts of honor
and caricatures of evil, dollars fanning from Uncle Sam's top hat.
Bread offered as resistance.
And when I ask her about *this time*, Eva says,
Of course, we are weeping!

Of course, we are weeping!

I tell Em, I will weep with anger.
I will listen to the trees calling from the ground,
the circle of hands surrounding us.
If I think I cannot speak, I will remember:
Of course, we speak.
Of course, we march in the road and sit down when the way is blocked.

This has taken my lifetime, long and longer.
To move forward and begin again
knowing
the need. Moreso.
Of course, we weep,
brush the ground, here and here, with our feet,
beside the shadow of our sister's
long standing
underneath.

Songs for Faerie Kingdom

Song for Ron
after Federico García Lorca's *Song of the Fairy*

The fairy arranges
his gray curls and beard,
brown eyes urgent,
playful in his proud, tall head.

The neighbors smile
as they see he works the field,
joke about Faerie Kingdom
from pale Chevy's and hot black trucks.

The fairy keeps his hands in the soil
impressing others as they natter on,
about Faerie Kingdom, his naked silence
and fear him, his capable hands.

In the barnyard, baby chicks peck, seek water,
while the young roosters plot moonlit revenge,
dead by daybreak, for any blood among them.

The fairy pretties himself
with nail polish—hands and feet—
and wears fairy rings, feathers and studs, makes his own kind
of signs for the many sweet pacts between men.
Only the sunflower, full of dropping seed, will remember
the upturned face, sunny sex becoming hungry mouth of sky.

Some days are harder, if the fairy turns
against love, or himself, for no reason.
The afternoon turns peculiar
if he thinks he is ugly as fools dare (him) to say.
He puts on his mask, loud as speech,
And wears his true beauty as mirror to the world.

A mask for a male goat pretending to be a turnip

Let me stop the ravenous clearing—
chewing alder, raspberries, all and whatever's left!
Let me rock on all fours, balls
steaming, and twitching tail too!
Let me summon my goat
into my white pointed beard

and drop like a carrot into the ground.
Funnel front legs, then rear, and pale belly down!
Let me stay in one place
to grow from what comes
from above, from below with horned head bowed
to root crops under my split hooves sown.

A mask for a rhinoceros praying to the moon

Oh Moon skull flying!   Oh Moon skull shining!
How can I reach you?
You who have taught me to love my small old eyes

How can I sweep your pitted brow
with my tender horn as I wade in rivers, sink in shyness?

How I raise my horn as delicately as a feather to you
in shadow, in shadow, my hide
swallows light in dusty rivulets
and my slick face shines.

Birds rest on my back
move up to my skull
then fly from my skull.

I have learned a few things:
my small boned friends told me
about living on the desert
when time and tide were one and how they too
had horns for beaks and hides under feathers.

Oh Moon skull flying!   Oh Moon skull shining!

My tusk cannot praise the cold sky, sorrow moon,
and small eye knowledge
held in the desert
of my face.

A mask for a stone trying to be discovered

Unbutton my slate-colored eyes:
I see well below the surface.
I respond to water like nothing else.

I can feel it coming:
high tide and hurricanes churn me up.
I love a good storm!

The next wave could be the one
where I tumble, one among many:
a pile of rocks!

How I dream of landing.

Early Days

Fog lay on his feet.
He couldn't see the ground
breathing all around him.

He felt the high hill under his boots, unseen
fifty-mile view to the Camden Hills.

The hill would farm well—old Cape facing east.
The house stood, windows gone
where the shotgun hit,
after the clan came back
and laid it to rest, leaving
blast holes to the sun.

Made sure the old place was shot clear through,
taken care of, dead. House with no windows
or doors, taken down to nothing, basic
respect for what's gone, no family left.

The faerie begins making
all he touches new.
Alder thickets clear, sky
dome: the first color, blue.

I Give You Stories

At 50, he said: I'm done farming.
I worked for free my whole life.
I don't want to keel over at 60,
already dead from standing.

When he walked away, he stayed a queer activist,
worker bee who weaves his many-threaded love.
Always a weaver, he plans
how to thread silk—black on the weft,
purple in the harness, treadles pink / blue
sheen as the horizon passes through his fingers.

Ron gave himself
more time.

Brother Dennis leaves the farm for good after the stroke.
His first words, 'I give you flowers.'
Dennis speaks 'I give you,' now.

Flowers tell nothing, just grow
from the ground
to the sun
like the young brothers
back on the Michigan farm.

His mother told him he was different
and he spends the day knitting,
learned at five by her side
where he was safe and hid his height in her apron.

Ron's the one left who lives his own life,
south side of his Cape bannered IMPEACH.
He feels the sun on the hill in Penobscot
where he lives in the place he named Faerie Kingdom.

At 66

And here I am wondering at 66
how to handle the decisions on booking travel, broken down
into one-week increments, and where I can
afford to go, and where I have to go.

And I get a call from SOCIAL SECURITY! on my new, year-ago cell phone
telling me that not only has my filing for retirement benefits
been approved (at 66),
but that I can collect for the two months
previous,
when I was eligible for benefits,
having turned 66 in October.

And just an hour ago, I was on the Woman Within site
plus-size, and wondering if
I could buy a new sports bra for my new job
and looking at the long, black v-neck cashmere blend cardigans
which looked pretty elegant and could be kind of funky too.

And next, this woman with the gorgeous voice calls from Maryland
as I'm turning to the day's work in my comfy squashed-cushion chair,
looking up Baldwin's exact words
about learning to love and knowing how very hard that can be,
especially in the face of hatred
and delusion, but the only way to get
White American men to face themselves, and learn to love and not hate, is
to get them to look at history. Then it is possible... perhaps.
And how we have to learn to love.

And this woman with the gorgeous voice calling from Maryland
and not mispronouncing my first name says she's from Social Security
and tells me that I will receive
the two additional months
I am due
for $1887.80
in about a week, direct deposit.
So I say, God Bless Social Security!
and in her good Black, Maryland accent, she says, Well, Thank You!
and she means it

and then a full-throated, And God Bless You!

I received her good tidings and told my mother who has been around a lot
    recently
and who had appeared in my dreams last night in the driver's seat
of a Winnebago we were sharing on a road trip,
since I was moving somewhere south and maybe across the country.
She said she knew that some good things were coming down the pike
and couldn't I feel it? We had both been sleeping in the dream
and she woke up in the front of the Winne camper
and was ready to get going as soon as i woke up...
But now she's asking me again, didn't I feel it? Wasn't that why
I decided I had to buy a new phone last night, because I needed it,
and some things were changing
and this was going to be one of them—
getting hip to my needs.

And in fact, for three days last week, I got hip to my needs and started
waking up smart and jumping out of bed to do what I wanted
like walking in the fog and cooking, besides the rest,
and maybe, thanks to acupuncture and maybe, thanks to less allergens in the air,
what with the downward temps, and maybe just
because.
I had been in the overwhelm story all fall,
and maybe all summer, and maybe just too damn long all around,
I began filling out my social security forms online for my retirement
benefits, nervous or not.

I had researched my situation, so I knew this was the right thing.
And I saved all of the answers on the forms and went over them
for three nights after work,
until I thought it was okay or provisionally ok, or until proven otherwise, ok.

But I was not yet pushing the button.
And I spoke of my fear of forms with friends who didn't mind,
and about my always wondering
too much and not always able to answer, until the third or fourth re-read,
because
I am always wondering
something
else.

And today, I am feeling like saying God Bless Social Security!

and feeling the edgy tones of June Jordan and Bobby Dylan and my mother too,
because they are sharp, and I am grateful to have them on my side. Dead or alive,
the message is clear. They all want to help me
with their good sense, extra dream sensing and in singing a song
for Social Security
and not caring, if it is ridiculous, or what!
Because it is profound and just in time,
social security.

Outpost

I am religious
about lying—
Do not lie and yes, sometimes fear,
old coat, tries to drape my shoulders,
but speaking, it turns out, is a friend,
the raw blunder necessary

even without an I or how to make a sentence
clear   I have taught some
grammar, composition
and "they was outback talking" is clear enough.

It matters, I tell them. All of it.
Their stories and the others. I ask them to think
about a time when they will be asked
to communicate life and death instructions,
something very important
to someone they do not know
who speaks a different language from their own.

Together, they have to come up with
(and you should know that you always repeat
the most important part of a sentence in New England)
life and death instructions
for the rest of us, whoever we may be.
Those two, just *those two,*
will be the last outpost
for relaying news to the rest of us.

You might ask how two
people could be an outpost—
Well, who else better? And may they
better share the language
of birds.

In Maine, there's a chance
they will see It coming,
because of all that time spent outback.

It feels like years.
And no clock.

The Balm of Friendship, 3/10-12/20

I always have a NYC layover after the MFA residencies for needed sleep, given the time change, and ground on my old turf. I stay in the same building on the Upper West Side where I see my old, close friends and renew the balm of friendship.

Hello – o! E. enters the apartment and places yogurt, raspberries, blueberries on Sal's worktable in the living room. All the surfaces at Sonia and Sal's are for art, a few eating spots, or covered with books—open today to the painted Greek icon, Mother of God of Tenderness, the Holy Virgin and her son Jesus; and under the lamp, Ravenna's Byzantine mosaics in Basilica of San Vitale.
We need to be careful of Sal's stuff.
I know, I know. I live here, you know, 50 years in the same building! You know who found them this apartment.
Yes, of course – I just remember when we ate here last month and hadn't cleared the dishes off, when he arrived from upstate –
Is he coming?
No, they're upstate – Sonia's got a cold, Sal broke his toe plus the insanity. They want to avoid the crazy-
What craziness? It's NY.
This thing–you know, the Corona virus. I get two blue plates down.
I'm not hungry –
Fine. I'm serving up some borscht.
A no-thank-you portion—
Fine and toasting a bagel— I have hummus.
I just want yogurt.
Fine. I'll be right back. I put a large portion of borscht in one bowl, place an empty underneath and stack the bowls on the plate and bagel to the side. There!
I'm not really hungry
Fine. I lather some hummus on a corner of the half bagel and hand it to her. Try a little borscht?
Cold?
Yes.
Good.
I serve the borscht by the teaspoon into the bottom bowl.
That's enough.
I hand her the bowl, I spoke to Sonia. I'm sorry to miss her this time.
Oh?
She's not coming in.
Oh, why not? She coughs, clears her throat in a neighing sound.
They're staying upstate to avoid the craziness.

What craziness?

You know, the virus.

Oh. She coughs and brings up phlegm, wipes a Kleenex across her lips.

Sonia has a cold too. Sal broke his toe.

He did?!

Yeah, he's got a boot.

And what about Sonia?

She's staying upstate.

No class at Hunter?

She cancelled and next week is the break. Have some borscht.

E takes some teaspoons, a bite of bagel. This is good. I haven't had this in a long time.

Zabar's.

Ahh. This is *very* good borscht.

The last container of soup. It's all beets. We can't go for coffee—

The last?

Everyone's shopping for soup, stocking up. No Zabar's for morning coffee –

Always good, borscht. No Zabar's?

No, the virus.

She looks glum but eats more bagel, more hummus. The dark purple soup has a density and holds still in the spoons. We lift spoons and smile across the bowls.

I pass more bagel with hummus to E who is quiet eating, and she takes it in her hand. She wears five rings on one hand and three on the other—the Norwegian spiral with her mother's Mexican silver ring with the circles within the rectangle, and an ornate Victorian winged setting of smoky green stone on her index finger.

Once we bought copper and brass twined rings as the simplest gesture of our domestic partnership at City Hall with the two of us laughing in the crowd of people waiting to get married— some clearly thrilled with milling family crowding for pictures, and others, clearly immigration marriages, stiff and trying to look friendly.

We were not allowed in the chapel, and shrugged, *as if,* to each other. Who knows where those rings are now, but she probably has hers.

Her green earrings clack, the wooden grooved feathers slapping together as she leans forward – her green jacket with scalloped collar over a black shirt with a necklace of crystal, silver beads and black spiky chunks of metal below the collar. Her hair is almost all gray, some brown peeking through loose curls, her brow finally lined– eyes large, questioning and sometimes, slightly mystified, surprised by what is occurring around her, staring a bit longer.

But she's a New Yorker, 83 or 84, unfazed, with Mexican paternity.

I am 12 or 13 years younger, depending on the time of year. It always mattered– and now, more than I ever dreamed. I repeat the basics—sometimes, feeling trapped by repetition, a robot. It can drive me crazy, repeating facts–and why should facts dictate everything? It can be oddly comforting. A flattening of all events into one stream. Does it matter?

When we take walks, we see things change together. Like the newest leaves on the bushes by the lake in Central Park, the crocus on the winding side path where I assure her some young guy sitting on a log isn't going to hurt us.

It's still light. Look at the Snowdrops, the runners at the end of the path–

She laughs, Still lots of people trying to stay fit, and others, she gestures with her head as we pass a chunky dad who doesn't look like a big exerciser who's holding a child by the hood, a pink fleece bunny hat draping into a coat, to keep her upright. She's just beginning to walk, E says.

The child's legs stick the air and her feet roll, wobbly on landing. First steps in the park and the child, eager to get to more people, the lake, quacking ducks.

We nod at these signs of spring everywhere around us.

When we rushed to the eye doctor earlier, E said she had shortness of breath. I tell her daughter about it: Her cough is worse. I only see her every few months, so perhaps I notice more.

She's glad I noticed the cough before this time, tells me she has a plan. If she gets sick: they'll take her at the hospital, because of her history.

I've been here before.

I keep thinking about E saying, she can't afford to get winded. And yes, we were rushing – What if I don't see her again?!

E. has finished her bowl and moves to clean up – always first to carry plates to the sink, fighting other people away, whether two or a feast of diners.

Hey, there's a live stream tonight of Simone Dinnerstein at the Miller— the Bach program.

I was going to go.

They canceled – the virus, but they're playing.

How? I had a ticket…

We can listen.

I was going to go.

I click the Miller link, and there she is at the piano, Simone Dinnerstein, musicians circled around her—violins, cellos, an oboe and a singer.

All Bach program, the Head of the Miller is talking about staying connected through music.

E makes a face – kind of making a fuss—no?

It's because of our situation

So?

The virus.

Oh.

The playing begins –Dinnerstein leaning into the piano, the crown of her head pushing the air, swooping over her hands with her torso. Her fingers have the same shape, equally muscular. The strings, the oboe—how the oboe twines them all together, and Dinnerstein leads them to the center, Bach rising above her and the piano.

Look how the camera gives such a wonderful view, E says, her eyes lit. Better than being there!

They are full into the familiar, *Jesu, Joy of Man's Desiring*. We await the young singer—

statuesque, eyes outlined, painted lips wide. And I wonder what it's like to dress for the part – the bright make-up, vibrating shell housing the voice. To bring it all to the surface with her voice.

She's a mezzo soprano, E offers.

So beautiful, I smile, and E. smiles back bathed in the music.

I have enough, E. translates the German, the final words of the most performed of the sacred cantatas, *Ich habe genug*. Or perhaps, *I am content*, she raises her eyebrow. She of six languages, all related in some way, and I realize she knows more about Bach than I ever will.

Jean here—

Leaving them rough without tearing
I wrote pages seeing you at the window
gleaming

Tonight, pages shift
darkened by eclipse
blowing clouds blowing across
a waxing Moon
corner and curve taken
off remains bright

Eclipse
seeping pink edge into dark,
a hunted feeling
peepers soft braying

Is that you the sheer
strong mist murmuring
to the Moon

I feel the poem
change since you
are not outside
You are inside

How human
cries a grief color
I wrote waves

where you might lay a night flower
or a bead on a stone
or rain necklace of mist
for the throat

The hollow place where the moon bleeds
and battered becomes beauty, eclipse
red with life
glow coming out of cold

Naming the Source

M is proving not asking
where to find the evidence
he knows holds true.

He views the contents of the libraries, unveils the Latin
and all predecessors—stark comparisons—
like the trees without leaves, their dark rings and scarred bark,
swaying with relief in the early spring season
finding themselves in altered air:
they are visible to themselves across time.

What is it to see across time?
Can we ask the trees?
Can we see between like the light?

The width of sun in the forest: how the deepening
green canopy is lit without shadow.

What began as a language of trees,
alone and in agreement from winter,
became a place where as Mahmoud said about hyacinths in Iraq—
the same stalks curled with white blooms, now slightly rotting
in the place where he sat in the New Hampshire library,
when I asked about what flowers grow there… he exclaimed, all senses
alert, do you know all the flowers of the world
were born by seed in Iraq?

There is no comparison
but the spread of flowers,
the evidence of flowers.

Her Late November

Meena, I had to tell someone we both love.
I came back to the room, plants pressed to the glass,
listening to the 79th Street rush below. The pomegranate in the kitchen,
orange cranberry dusk, children's voices rising from the schoolyard.
My hand went to the pomegranate: we could share this, for Meena.

Electa came in, two bag wrist dangle, bracelets, beige and bright green
weights, the usual fist of papers. Her rebozo around her shoulders, black wool
tassles almost touching the ground as she relayed her conversation with an Indian
man working at the Lebanese Deli on the corner across the way: *He was telling me
about what it meant—Partition—for him growing up. He was born in 1951
in Islamabad.* Meena was born in 1951—her signal touch
tapping in to your corner of the world
before you had to hear the news.
Meena brought evidence of remembering—the split, the music of
split language you both shared, and the talk that can bring it all
back, alive on the streets of the City. Meena's musical
being, at play in the hallway.

You taught, side by side in more than one tongue, and became
changing face and motion sliding over the plates under the sea:
Indian Ocean, Mediterranean, Gulf of Mexico and the Atlantic.
You wrung fever and sweet release from leaping waves of grief,
danced through healing hybrid waters to a binding sisterhood,
Mexico and India, recalled as one, same, different. You received eager students,
women who noted how you draped the bright-stitched black shawl,
and how you bound the gold sari to align flesh and memory,
calling power to arrival, color flowing ahead or behind, down the hall.

I had to tell Electa, someone we both love: Say it, *Meena died.*

Everything left her hands—dropped, flung away—she who always holds more—
pen, pencil, hardback, paper, sprouting unwritten and eager
to-be-read, different continents, grief of storied exile, from the bone back to music.

She flings away, *Meena*—name sung, singing—
Her fingers open and the web of flesh cut between the fingers, hurting.
She spreads her empty hands.

Words dropped in the hallways of New York,
here on the polished brown parquet floor.

None of this makes any sense.
How can these torn oceans flow between?
The tide comes down the hall remembering this morning.

We had been talking about pomegranates
and whether they can be called seed or flesh.
How to describe the bulb, the seed, the many:
pumped red, tiny tongues of hidden speech.

Was that you, Meena, playing with names,
talking about hidden forms of joy and sorrow,
holding the shadow turned, as Persephone faded,
her fingers reaching for flesh and blood relation,
her mother carrying the seed of devotion
into memory: never separate, never one.

The pomegranate bears fruit
in two hemispheres and the inner fruit
cannot begin to say how the world is divided.
It is all one flesh in the seeds.

We have entered the season of fruit, Meena.
The pomegranate will make a tower for you with hard, lit bulbs,
colored soft orange to cranberry red. Not blood.
That will be saved for the taste of your words.

We fling the years against the wall, burst the ripe fruit
to fill the porousness, just holes. Meena died.

A chill—feast table of sorrow gathering home in her late November.
A desire for sweetness on the tongue, a word.

It all seems so long ago, and just then, rising salt on the tongue,
and her golden color inside loose inner sleeves,
our arms brush the silk as her body turns.

Winter Summer

for David & Royce, 6/29/22

In a passageway headed home, David comes towards me, Royce close
behind, still walking through the dying time. White walls.
No place, name or transportation.
Walking. Just walking.

I dreamt your face large, David,
grayed after your sister
passed. Your forehead washed
pale, ears too, and color
beginning below your dark brow,
flickering bright eyes.

Her death rose from your head, scalp
and kept pulling away, wanting to show itself
as fact, pale beside the living
and as we hugged in a return
passage, white walls, I felt your fingers
holding tight below my shoulder blades, digging in a bit
to realize flesh and bone, and hold on. I felt how
your frame was lighter, the bones smaller than I thought.

Pulling back, part absent, hatchwork
of shadows, it was clear you knew
she had left her life. Some color
from your face—childhood resemblance
or tone of voice, the blood things
had gone with her. You would
change too, but the mark, the draining
of color from the face, called
momentary, had touched you.
You absorbing death—not yours, hers—
as you re-entered your life in a kind of winter
summer where the colors trailed unopened below
the ground, not knowing quite when to bloom
or where to show their faces.

Your July

    1.

You survived him

The shock cracked the shell and emptiness, a blade of light,
kept coming through your shell, Cancer, tracing bone hollows
and light gashes for another nine months
before you died in spring, the final bleed of light
let through

    2.

You survived him

Always a new feature to the story and the lines
warming my face as they get closer together

Now that we
are the ones
left, we stayed
alive for you

You thought the same way.

The longer, the better.
and no hope reproducing more
than death.

    3.

You weren't afraid.
Met the empty before.
You taught us
full face.
Not to be afraid.

How to live is the question

still preying
waxing in July.

Yours, early for blooming,
late for skeptics.
Your July.

    4.

Nothing new
as the day disposes of clouds
and invents a floater.

No one would've thought
you could've created
such resilience
in your children. But loyalty
teaches persistence.

You met shock of cloudless blue
and no one looking back.

More blue.

You had your reasons
for distrust
and they returned
to show themselves.

You didn't live to see the familiar
turn to hatchet
but we knew by virtue of all your warnings
how to become wood, so that what seemed
an easy target
could become a tree
and keep growing.

Knowing how to do this is some trick.
You knew the worst might be coming.
We learned that from you.
It could always happen. That wouldn't change
with or without clouds peopling the sky.

Or a jealous fall, clear and cold,
rain pounding fruit asunder to rot and empty
flesh into the ground, into the widening dirt
before covering the face turned hard with snow.

The pines release it all
to the ground, dropping
the weight of held cold
across slippery needles
and sprouting infinity.

5.

Flexibility is in the trees,
shallow hand across rock
or deep mirror tap root.
Sacrifice the fruit for the tree.

Today, the urge for widening into warm is ours,
our just July is here.
To be alive.

Not a breath of wind
on the water. Sun rising wide
July, ready for a run towards August
and holding enough back to turn the heads
of flowers, those steadfast
around you still growing.

Resistance

She heard it from her bed
where she heard most of the conversation
about her life leaving. From downstairs
coming up, she'd heard her daughter on the phone
checking agencies for help, the cost, for shifts—
a nurse for an overnight, a regular
for four days a week or three.
She had resisted, even as she heard her daughter
interviewing people on the phone. Getting information
just as she would. But she only wanted family,
her daughter, her son.
No one else. No intrusions.
She had not dismissed it, nor agreed.
She knew they were tired, but she wanted them
close. Her own witnesses. To her life.
She was still alive. She was not letting death in.
That's what help meant, the admission.

What was that sound?
Her son had gone out. He tried not to smoke in the house–
a reminder of his father's cancer.
Nine months to the day, since David died.
In the Navy, crossing the Atlantic in the War.
The Mediterranean, The Canal. The Gulf and back. All that water.
The men–boys really as he described them lining up for inspection
in ill-fitting helmets. He felt for their youth and told her about them in letters.
He was 12 years their senior, committed, married.
With the Captain locked in his bunk, drinking,
David, next in command, managed the tasks and orders for him.
Gunner, testing guns on deck and running training practice,
he was minister on Sunday, mail censor and disciplinarian.
It's a wonder he hadn't turned to drink.
They all smoked.

She heard it again—a sound like an inhale—
chesty, muffled.
Was it a cry?
She wiped her brow with the cool washcloth
by the bed and dried her hands on the towel–the nubbly

small towel. Someone was crying into a towel.
It was coming from the bathroom across the hall.
The oddly shaped room made into a bath,
big enough to be a bedroom—that's what happens when you chop
these old houses up. Once a house, now three apartments.
Thank God, they couldn't hear the others next door.
The sound stopped.
She heard the door to the bathroom open, a click.
It was her daughter.
There was nowhere else for her to go.
Her daughter crossed the threshold.

She brightened at the sight—her lean figure and honey-colored hair,
her pleasant expression, David's dark blue eyes.
She had a lot of him in her, but she was emotional. Her daughter,
determined, kept it in check, until she didn't.
How they had fought.
Under the surface her daughter roiled, grieved.
It came to her easy as the breeze
coming through the window, "I've decided you can get help. Come sit."
She reached towards her daughter who gave
both hands to her, under her mother's smaller palms
knees touching the coverlet.
"You have your father's hands."
"Yes."
"It's a good thing."

Another mother, my own:

B: Mother—You, really my mother

M: Yes always

B: I cannot believe I have pushed you so far away

M: I am here   Always

B: I will not make you the same

I want to feel you
person
How do I do it?

To tear away sounds that ricochet, hurting
The knife-sharp smallens Not see
Not feel

M: They are not alive   I am here
They words   they go, aloud, yourself ricochet

But grief is loud and soundless—
many shouted raw
choked in throat cried undercloud
prayed and whispered in the hairs of tangle mouth
lunging away
Grief, Yes

Loss will fall

Touch my hands
I am here

I will not flinch   I promise you

I heard it all before and into the disappearance

It is changing
I am always here

B: And how can I become   allow the place of wound to go

M: It's not the same for me

I have no anger

I have a peace, a place to hold a quiet
Soothing
A place without harm
I can show you

B: I don't know if I can get there
Is it hard as what came before?

What will be left?

M: No, it is not the same.
Pain comes and goes in what life you and I have known

This is different knowing
having known pain but not in pain
The knowledge is there, not erased – known—
The turmoil   strain of blows
falls away

The clarity of the star
clarity of a nestled diamond
nested shining brightness

It is how we are made
Love emerging inside the chest
made of the same stuff
as stars a yearning shared
We are made the same
Always

We do not have to close
to close the wound

Let it be large and speak

You are part of me

Here, pulse!
Our blood,
the stars

Last night

Last night, I turned away from the beautiful. My beautiful dying horse. He had been hit by a moving vehicle, something larger, hurt. He was lying on the ground, breathing, and my fear of death, being beside it, was large. Then a clear urge to be there to kneel beside the dying horse, his big darkening green head and muscled chest, chestnut body. The eyes knew me, a sweet relieving exhale as I took the head, rubbed the jaw and long veined nose.

I would not hurt, I would help. Looking straight ahead, soft knowing and forgiving my waiting: I watched and watch the dying change color to become real.

Yes, here: the horse knew about me, my arriving to be there to the end, his calm and changing before my eyes. Full thank you, dear witness of the darkening shade pulling down, eyes straight ahead. I have lost and found my place next to you. Dying, loving, being and being loved.

The horse is true.

Later morning, I tell the young man, my old friend's grandson on the phone translating for her in her deafness: I love your grandmother very much, and that means I love you too. He understands, *Yes*, he says, *I send it back to you.*

Yes. Loving means loved.

How to be carried in my shadow, March to April

for Marie in April

How to be carried in my shadow
when the wind is cracking air from ice
and there the mirror gone.
Tongue unleashed its last year stub.

Ground uncovered, stone alive—broken, bald or split.
Trees stripped and bloom (in its own imagining)
defies all shades of gray.

Earth welcomes movement, to hear the trees surrender:
A row of swaying pine touch in the west,
the ones I watch like brothers
and sisters all year, inside the forest I stand small in.

It's only the sky that blues and greens,
nothing more with wind in charge.
The sky comes down
to blue between the stony toes of March
and pulls a comb through clotting mud and sticks,
the pelt of moss and melting cries
of stone cold sweat and upturned sight.

Carried through nights of dreamy ash,
dying fires and me, we wake on the other side
of bed, talk to spears of light and curving quiet.

Shadow ground softens. I feel
the give: my body, a cloud growing limbs
dissolving snow.

Pull down   pull down my feet in spring.

The fish moon's coming,
then the velvet rain.

Skull Talk

Is there a cellar poem? How will I sing the cellar poem?
I almost knocked my block off when I fell, head hit
granite, a slab three feet wide,
not cut stone but a chunk – maybe the largest existing rock
in the ground, dug out to find the cellar and make it the base, dirt dug
with stone sides packed, rising, but this one rock – perhaps it could not
be moved and became the center from which all the rest balanced
as true as could be. And true: it did not kill me.

It was later in the week when I found the double axehead on the slab.
Had I seen it before? I was so appalled, perhaps I did not pick it up to look carefully
the first time, but decided it was an axe blade and let it go. But this week
I inspected it, turned it over, the weight of the labyris, the double axehead. It lay there
just above where my head hit, in shadow, beside the wooden pillar support going from
the center of the dirt cellar to a center beam behind the stairway's descent. A quick path
to heaven or forms of support to the rescue. A double axe that would've split me wide-
open without elaboration. Bloody—how it would've turned a notch from the weight
of the fall, the skull dropping back, or maybe stuck in my neck vertebrae, slicing partly
up the side of the ear and into the skull, not crushed but blood and bone fragments
running across the granite into the dirt of the cellar —the first dirt of home. Now, my
home.

Instead, after I fell, I rose slowly, felt the back of my head and no blood moisture but
the hurt as I ascended every step saying, *this fucking hurts, this fucking hurts,* until hand
to freezer door and all those freezer bags for arms wrists back hip at hand. I rolled two
inside a long dry towel, wrapped my head tight, knotted center above my eyes
and called my neighbor who was just going out. Caught her
and asked for her to stop, so we could gage together where to go.

I called my Health Center and asked, where should I go – they said you need an EKG, so
likely Ellsworth. My neighbor came and I told her the news and we were off in her car to
Ellsworth.

After the EKG, showing no fracture and no bleed at the moment, I was encouraged
to return, if I had a headache or any feelings of nausea. It was a half hour drive there
and back without traffic. Flood of relief and I forgot to ask anything else –having
pictured myself in hospital for a week of observation. I was given a sheet which I only
read a week later and luckily some friends told me that a mild concussion needed to
be watched and cared for, and that I should rest and rest, longer than I might think. I

did not realize how out of it I was, until three or four days in –still cooking for myself and resting, but not lying down all the time, listening to the radio in my wing chair and streaming some shows, I begin to notice that I was deep in.

When I went outside and sat in the clear air, the October sun, my attention was there where I sat looking down at the grass, the miracle of all those strands growing from the mat of the earth in the warm sun, a vast nest every which way, a network of grass and creatures, insects climbing falling making their way ants and spiders and next to me or across my arm or down my chair. How the spiders hesitated, how they dropped, how they lifted on the breeze away from whatever objects they were attached to and how they leave the grasses and rise up the side of the turned-over wooden box. How the spider flew on the air to the next station, swinging in space or easily landed by one leg touch. How they worked and did not work. How to fly and how to let go and land became the question. I had no anxiety and only a shuddering failure of any thought that brought too much to bear or any action that brought too much for my body. When my whole body said No and knew what it was talking about. I was not worried, I was very defined within a floating space. It was quite wonderful and wondering.

I felt the skull. Warm wormy trails, squiggly flashes all around my head. It felt good, some kind of nerve blood. Inside my cap – capping my skull, not brain waves, but squiggles on a map or handwriting nerves. It was not something I knew–finding my nerve again—it was something that was happening. Finding it again. Kind of exciting–friendly and part of me, without thought, no agenda.

As I got better and I slowed—doing one day resting and the next, some work. Never two days in a row, I noticed a slow gathering. Some anxiety crept in as if it was a cap that could be taken on and off, or thrown aside, but it was present peeking out from the hat rack.

The idea of driving was not my favorite, but I tried. I took a short trip to the Post Office—usually about 12 minutes – and I was totally terrified the whole time.

It was because I was floating still, adrift, and the idea that I knew that motion across and down the road, going this fast as if it was normal, was foreign to me. I knew I had known how to do this, but at the moment, it was all brand new and terrifying. I drove very slowly.

A few days later, deep in the long end of summer day, I drove to a meeting at the school. I was terrified but not quite as much. I drove slowly. On the drive home, it felt easier. To accept the insanity of driving a car. I drove slowly.

I remember when I first learned to drive thinking it was insane to go through these mechanisms, and make motions within the machine, as if it was all easy and fine. To drive along without noticing other humans and other cars with sights moving by. And other hearts and their troubles and all their loves acting as if nothing mattered except driving down the road, that was crazy. It seemed to me insane. How could I ever not know what else was driving me down the road?

Yet this time I saw that the forgetting was being able to drive. I began to let myself forget and I drove slowly. I wondered when I began to drive faster, if I was getting better or just getting crazier. I drive more slowly now. Period.

When I drive more slowly, I know that wonder sits inside, kept by craziness at the door. I went through a door down the cellar stairs and as I slipped on the way back up, caught my elbow on the open stair and swung myself towards the hoses underneath the stairs, because I knew the pile of lumber nearby had nails. I missed the nail clad lumber and for a second, felt the coiled roll of hose under my back until my head tipped back and found the granite – perhaps the first stone laid for this house built in 1835. But the house has always liked people, and liked me, and it was as it happens the birthday of a dear relative, so perhaps the house encouraged my quick athletic response—my left elbow, the one with tendinitis, would rescue me. And my dear cousin who had passed was there with her birthday light. And my wanting to do right, my desire not to fail at living here in the deep north of New England. Some pride in the moment, and some patience learned without pride and despite it, let me live and go on to see more and to see less. The grass and the insects living in the sun, living and working.

Dear Settler Settling,

First, skeleton and flesh,
M says, and the space inside
and outside the body.

I search my computer
for the final
versions—
I, without the contents
    of the book at hand.
I think of you as one who holds it all
    inside—while it is not coming all out yet right.
I search for the right words,
    find old versions—know they hold
less, more than I have in front of me.

Is this what it's like for you
    revising sentences mid-air
    to make the sense you know
    we can hold.
You see the rest of the words
    giving way or (explicitly) not there.

You tell me you see
    pale yellow in spaces
    where words are not
    in three parts:
the first, present.
the second, present.
the third, not there.
The sentence does not end
    as you know it
given into speech.

The nick took—lit the wick: you received
the right treatment within the first
two hours, the doctor having a cigarette on break,
then back in just as you arrived.
Perfect timing—the smoke,
the knife, the bloodflow nick.

You describe your world as smaller
and just right. You accept the sentence
   without an ending as the perfect answer
      of naming you and you and me
in the experience of skeleton and flesh
being spoken here
and (which) not all of us get.

Walking with a Friend, Blood in Our Hooves

for Bhanu

Across the Straits of San Juan de Fuca, Victoria's purple mass.
We have let talk go, stopped taking pictures
as the ghost ship begins to stitch the opposing shore.
Subs belly down through the Strait—
eight Tridents locked in below the Canal.
Orcas carve the waters, pod breaching led by mothers, guarded
by grandmothers, golden lip closing on darkness at sunset.

Breaking a hard year by breaching trouble, twisting away,
and diving below the line, my friend
changing the definition of above and below, churns
water into wake.
What is it to open to the waves and what they say?
She will be on the current today:
forks of fish inside churls of cold, birds spearing shine.
She has to go below to mouth the words and scream
unblocking passageways of adversarial currents
to meet herself without burden
of need for safe harbor or anchor.
She is taking her ground back.
Strength, not needing more.
Not needing.

In the open field on the path back, we let two men go ahead,
let their smoke and talk train, as we fall
into a single line, as they pass.
These two—a tall, weedy older white man,
beaten down, tired like a worn pocket, something dangling from his belt.
And the thick legged, younger pal leading with his cap.
Through the meadow to the forest,
Madrone and Pine, and the path home.
They stop abruptly by scrubby trees, gawk at a three-point buck—
rust fur glossing new antlers. We do not stop,
walk by, glad to have their focus trained on the buck
as we head into the forest, leave them staring, hands loose at their sides,
at this, their unsought prize.
The buck is young, unused to what he is carrying on his head
even as he grows into his crown.
We are freed to feel tree roots, smell Blackberry earth, as the buck's daring

guards the field, our journey inside the darkening wood.
We traded places, walking through a fearful air
and into the golden glow. We held the beating blood in our hooves.
Any threat in the air around us, reason enough to run.

Across the Strait, across the specifics
of difficulty,
trouble, distress
perplexing and paralyzing.
You've seen it. We all have.
The subs just above the surface.
Across the straits
visible invisible,
perplexing, if still kept secret,
immeasurable difficulties of our lives.

We face the sun.

The path back through the meadow,
the two men smoking, going ahead.
Should the two frighten us?
Younger man, pale, dusky haired, thick-legged, unsunned
wonders aloud about bike paths. Older man, beaten down, poor white,
torn pants. They walk and smoke as if they're not used to being outside
and the habit came with them, when they were released into air.

How are these two frightening to a brown woman and a white
woman walking in the field? Is one woman more interesting
to these two? One older, lesbian.
One brown, one white: is that interesting to them?
Is that why we need to be scared?

Do I want to be invisible? How can I be? I act big like the green frog the other day
when I touched him—puffing up to be larger and throw off threat.
I speak in jocular lingo repeating phrases like an older auntie.
The younger man asks about a bike path again. My friend says, she's never seen that.
I go into information mode, Ask at the park, on the other side of the woods.
As I say the other side, I remember how the path is blocked by uninhabited
    outbuildings.
I don't want them following us through the forest to the site.
It's out of the way. That kind of place is perfect to take us
and take us apart. I stop talking about the other side.
When we pass them, my flesh elongates flat against my bones to imitate thin steely

     nothing
or be mistaken for low brush beside the path flattened at the edges. I am part of an
impenetrable growth along the path. Nothing worth bothering with. Small bones
becoming branches. Strong bones I want hidden. I want to pass
as useless brush. I note my friend's deliberate step.

They turn into the field to see the young buck.
We walk above, aligned with the copper antlers.
If brown and white make copper, we are the shine
he sends from his glistening. His coat,
his proud curiosity in the air around him.
Shoulders alert, unmoving.
He has pinned the men in place
at the edge of the forest.

In my mind, we reach the orange mesh pulled across the woods path.
Do Not Enter, the deserted construction site at the end of the day.
I don't want to say more.
It's the kind of place where women
can be hurt.
Don't want to say words,
It won't happen
Not here, means *here*, once it happens.

The golden buck stands outlined in copper-threaded coat,
rust-colored antlers.
His thought is larger than all of us,
his bones, newly grown with bright blood
and black hooves hidden in the humped grasses.
He walked into the field
enlarging the vision.

The men: one tall, flagged to go soon; the second, short, learning to touch
the earth (hopefully) and walk in witness to the deer's strength.
This is the best we can hope for.

Two women carrying their lives in their hands.
One held a wand, a barnacled branch
drifted to the beach, an antler from the sea.
The other was becoming a deer.
What's long enough to wait
not having broken stride
before asking my friend as we inhale the rich fungal smells of the forest,

Were you frightened?
I waited to ask because I needed to keep my strength inside,
in case I needed the pent-up tension to tackle one of them.
The fear tracked us like the smoke wrapping around our shoulders.
She said, the older man didn't look that strong, but something was swinging from his
belt, a knife perhaps. His trousers torn. The other had strong legs, but she thought
the two of us could hold our own. She sussed it out. I thought perhaps I could talk to
the more talkative—lead him astray. The older one could not run far. You would run.
I would stay, easier for the white woman to face the white man and not be killed. I
thought I could undo him. And how
was this going to happen after we levelled the older man? Would the young man
find fury? I saw myself taking a pummeling.
How to fight–the position and limbs played out in our minds.
Without saying a word, we agreed we would survive.

The thought of the golden buck was ahead of us. He outlined
all there was to see–the limbs of the men
hanging limply in wonder at their sides –
the women walking strong and steady into the forest.
The buck made the pivot, stood and held it.
He could run and he could stand,
the women in the dark of the trees
and shadows. They were free to go
and the buck was free.

The Seep

There's a drought here in Maine, and lately I've been studying a seep in the backfield. A seep is a moist or wet place where water, usually groundwater, reaches the earth's surface from an underground aquifer and pools in a depression. A seep will be found quickly by wildlife and bring new birds and animals to the area. There is every sign that's true.

As for the drought, we're eight inches below normal rainfall, fire danger's high and there's trouble with a number of crops. Talking with Blaine Wardwell on his family's oil delivery route, I noted that the leaves on the apple trees were an early yellow. He said the trees will sacrifice the leaves for the fruit. The roots of the apple tree are deep and the orchards have needed watering, unheard of, or very rare. At the Blue Hill Public Library, the well ran dry. Striking in a small town, the library is a hub (a watering hole if you will) enjoying many steady customers, local and people from away. Having the well run dry was a constant reminder of the state of drought.

Safe, clean water is our most valuable, most necessary, and most threatened natural resource. Knowing how to find water is a skill and learning to sense the earth carefully is part of the skill required. Dowsing is an honored tradition and The Northern Maine chapter of the American Society of Dowsers meets every 3rd Saturday in Winter Harbor. I had watched the seep for years and assumed, wrongly, that it harbored a spring. Not so fast, it seems.

The verb *seep* sounds like itself, but as a noun, *seep* has a finality that water does not enjoy.

SEEP: seeped, seeping, seeps.
1. To pass slowly through small openings or pores; ooze: Water is *seeping* into the basement. 2. To enter, depart, or become diffused gradually: The importance of the situation finally seeped into my brain.

The message can arrive through an aquifer, slow and steady; and sometimes through another source disappearing, the smaller ways through become the lasting ways.

The seep is the place to start looking for change and steadiness, and this seep has been constant in the backfield, since I arrived on this land over ten years ago and long before. When the water line goes down extending the mud at the edge, the animal tracks are clear.

During the drought the seep has been an important source of water for the animals. Their footprints are all around the edges, small and large, deep and light, claws and hooves, wide pads and the drag of tails, visible as they come at different times of day to drink. I wonder how they find the seep. The information gets passed on, for sure. Is it the sound of water, or animal paths to the same spot gone over and matted down in the dark—one leading another? Is it the sound of the seep calling with peepers and frogs speaking from the muck? What is the sound of life in the muck?

Begin in a place of frustration and allow the forces around you to enter. Look for the footprints. You may be part of something larger. Community may not be where you think or expect.

Last week, a dear friend had a blood seep in her brain. She is out of danger now. They still don't know where it came from, the cause, but it has stopped. It could have been too much aspirin thinning her blood.

In this instance, the seep could have been fatal.

Communication was key and timing. The veins carried the information.

She's on the mend in New York City, thanks to her own quick call downstairs to a doorman who's the kind who can handle anything (Doorman who could be President). New York City smarts: Sit down, leave the apt door open, I'm calling 911. He then called her daughter, and the two of them rode to the hospital together. He saved her life.

The line to the desk downstairs, a vein in the communication aquifer, as is 911, and the trip to Lenox Hill within ten minutes: the procedure to drill a hole in her skull and drain the blood within minutes of arrival. The immediate gathering of loving and concerned around her, including the 24/7 ICU nursing.

What is intensive care?
A seep is dangerous. A seep is life giving.
And understanding between all the parts.

Now all the loving circle are on the same page.

All the animals have come to the seep to drink in the dark having heard the underground calling.

native tongue (1973-1976)

aside

why are you waiting
time straddled in your stance
overrun from somewhere, mud supporting your shoes -
your clothes have been worn beneath the feel
of time run smooth in your skin.
age moves outward you seem to say
                from your splintered core, or
that was just the wind,
        let it pass… sand's tongue dancing in your heel,
never shaken out.
you leave out more and more
as you become more and more the same
you wait for risk
        to take you up on yourself.

"conspiring to bless…"

you bear the thin airs of harvest.
from the most unlikely parts
you issue smoke.
your voice grazes the weeds
fraying the husk gold
feeding the gold twilight.

inside November

in two days the top leaves had turned hard as ochre.
a dark alarm that made me sure
the leaves would harden to wood
at the next evening of black wind.
the morning cold would slap any face proud
enough to poke around the screen door and hedge
by the dead flies at the feeling of intrusion
trading a warm breath then slamming
pink lungs shut.
the chimney is open and burning breath
as fast as it issues.
the chicken lie curdled in one body
warming the henhouse with insulting murmurs
that gurgle through the smooth slits
of white cracked winter light.

grandmother
for c.a.h.

old tree, your years are grace,
they have been moved.
in your own you took a dogged cat trail
through the cracks of pride
with mercy for this world.

our roof is soft, unfirm even,
for your step, and accordingly,
you touched less and less.
our possibility, newer than yours,
gathered around us unspecifically
and with haste.

i walked the roof tonight,
your branches tapped the edges.
i did not but cross
the clarity of your gaze.
i could not touch the same surface
as you reached towards me, warm palms

that last time, green touch, rings turned—
you saw it first,
look, look, the crocus
coming through the snow.

day of winter turning

for ann

1.

i sit in the room with the dark wood
yesterday, it snowed
lasting the night
today, i pass through it
i know in an instant:
i am a horse
the ground is true
i walk right by the day.

ll.

this is the room with the dark wood
licked by the leavings of afternoon.
by five, i can smell the rain
wax in the walls.
the light passes, what grace the disappearance has
i stare after it:
the windows, the blue glass, tin or midnight now,
each mile that falls away, each shrinking
skyless day.

dream: to my sister Elizabeth

to cg, dg and eg

the first died.
there were no pictures saved
but one turned up
curled in the corner of the seaman's chest
resting under the family
i picked it out
and saw my father's and my own gray eyes.
i watched her for a long time-
saw her hair go gray and fall light in the sun.
she was looking out a window—all the seasons passed
while she slowly counted
as if remembering the rains-
so unsought, her face.

Matt's Room: Looking Towards Mount Hunger, Monterey

There's a secret door here
     and a blooming window–
it greens open a little at time
    out over water.
The eye guts the air
     in half the time
it takes to dream a canoe
trip through the weeds below.
No, my skull opts for the sky
    and the open dive—
but here, halfway,
I am getting ready.
There's a pilot's cap on the peg.
Here, you must have wavered
    paced the room
    in the bomber jacket
tried the round glasses
     sat down, chased the idea—
nursing scotch, nursing heroes—
    steady Ferlinghetti
and the flight out.

for Gerard,

naked in the eye of the storm,
who burned it faster than the coal came
and grabbed the tail in the year of the dragon.

baja concepcione

the oldest screamings must coast like this
beneath the heat

the osprey has the fish already eaten
in the fix of his eye

the arroyo sleeps on purple air
and fallen mountain

the cactus picks his shape and lives there
against smooth roots and air

the wind tells stories of racing light
whipping shadows and aging with night

leaving the mountain at sunset
frigots fall like volcanic ash

the weight of all the rocks in the sea
neptune, bleak ages hushed by the tides

the tide lets the molten peaks out to the stars
black gold   bell anchor   silent   mountain boon

window

night blushes dark
velvet against the glass
as the cool dolor of the moon
spreads our limbs
bright across the bed.

native tongue
for bea

fire, the clinging : proudly.
you dress in torn air
and bring violence from the ground.
yr. sister of ash weaves
loose holes in the sky
directs yr. shadow to disappear
as she is
or has come to
be unknown in her share.
you take the same hydra ancestors
never having slept
past another's dream
or woken without hearing
the rising smoke of longing.

we walk from the fire.

Shooting at Night (1980)

In the Dark

Small wrists and large knuckles—
I make a fire and lay my hands down.
Twigs and boughs, paper
and the soft blowing on slow flame
ripping across newsprint.
I lay my hands down,
each finger a key to open or close
memory's marking in the palms.
Left what you are given;
right, what you make of it.
The hands pray
if only to meet as one.
The key slips from the hand
left or right   thrown away
in the snow   through the door.

Dream Pivot in the Night
for David

1

I am sitting—perhaps it's Sunday.
I see my brother outside
through the line of windows.
The white dog merciful by his side
the white dog I am glad to see.
My brother, broken and tired, clear rain
comes from his every pore—silhouette
cut sharp and ragged against the rain.
His hair is driving white,
shoulder blades peaked and smooth, wishbones
that fall in sharp angle to his fingertips—
white: sleet driving from his nails.
His knees rise and fall like needles
in the wet and past the last window.

2

I am at the door
welcoming, portrait of an arrival.
My brother's Chevy sits in the drive.
The windshield is gone,
a few crystals cling to the rubber seaming.
He sits in the driver's seat
both eyes shucked clean by the vision
of what has just passed in front of him.

The Visit

I float by the mirror.
I do not stay—
just my uneven breath on the glass.
I turn and hear the faded dresses
and fixed hats speak:
'Yes, you have the same forehead as your mother'
and the same tiny tearpocket
at the outer edge of the eye.
The real resemblance appears
without my knowing.

I move down the hall
float by the x-ray machine
follow the blotches on the screen
and lose them.
Slower I see they are my lungs,
red fish bobbing just below the surface—
strange survivors let loose to swim withing range—
the waiting eyes, the soundless feet
and the machine behind the glass.

Four women in separate beds—
the new one, the old one,
the one just out of surgery
and my mother, ready for release.
Four women watch each other.
The light and dark of their bodies
turns through the sheet,
piranhas hitting the sides of the tank.
The new one spills her dinner
and cannot move well around it.
"Get the coffee, she won't notice,"
I am instructed.
Instead, I lift her from her chair
and dry under her dress.
She's light as wicker threads let go—
"Stupid, stupid," she says.
My mother and the old-timer chime: "It's all right!"

A moan comes up—the one just out—
struggles, her hands tight to the bed,
to set her feet on the floor.
The deep bruised shadows open and close
on her face.
Her feet mysteriously
like the new-born
stretching just out of reach
of her slippers.

I gather the soft bundles and one suitcase.
My mother checks her mirror, nicks the sleep
from the corners of her eyes
and brushes the hair from her forehead.
"Don't walk in front of me.
Walk beside me."

Mrs. Cratty's Apparition

The paint cracks in fickle shards
keeps calendar of how long and how cold.
The wind whines outside, line after line,
the clothesline grows musical,
grows icicles, sows percussion
extending creak of beam.

Inside, a long-necked woman
bent to the silvery, peeling wall
large bulb of head askew, listens
to something begun—
lost track of where the cats are,
when she ate her last meal.

She is deaf and still—
still listening for the last word.
She knows it caught her with a shiny burst
knows she doesn't know
no gage—'til repetition
meets with her idea of things.

The high road still open inside her tulip skull,
her shoulders rained out and eroded
down to her glass stem.
Her strong eye knows and remembers—
the rhyme, the rhythm, the repetition.
She holds it all in mind
and beats it strongly with her claws
to break the spell and wonder
who ever heard such singing.

She sings alone and sings and weeps, repeats, repeats.

Translation of My Grandmother
for my mother

You spoke French and Italian
Russian and German
but somewhere something got lost
in translation, generation to generation.
Such gentleness for me in your eyes
while your own children grew
with little faith in words.

One knew the words for spade,
another, the one for rock
and the third knew to carve in stone
but they could not agree
where to bury you—

Your daughter heard the words,
hard as hail
on the glass of a nightmare:
ma mère, dans la terre, dans la terre.

Taunton Bay
for Charlie

Charlie's scar is buried
folded in deep below
his left cheekbone.
Bottle cracked on the stones
below his swift foot.
Brother quick
from the beach up the hill,
and younger sister pressed closer.

Blood on the beach
bones in the ground
ashes left a mark without a sound.

The scars are in the rocks and on the graves
above water and below the eyes.
The memory floats over our faces
as we meet and run together
on the river where you swim at night,
quiet one—*Remember me,*
warm heart and dry palms out.

The Balloonist
for my father

I recognize the man
in the balloon.
My father readies himself
moves carefully
and without alarm.
My disbelief hangs
in the air like smoke.
You know the necessity
of every movement;
unhitch the bags of sand.
Inhale   exhale
a trail of pale blue butterflies
rises in a stream from your lips—
the bruise of separation
begins at our feet on the ground.
I know the depth of your composure
as you loosen the ropes
and let your life go.

Esprit de Corps
for Rosa

Waking to a call
and fear of falling
through electric air
the night mares
loose across the sky.

I cannot tell
how the minutes die in front of us.
I watch them leave.
I cannot tell how we will change.
We are changing now
into next time
and the time after.

In the language of the dying
whose breath is the passageway
to the source, o singing heart,
so loud and proud
with each day.
It is a wonder
we are still alive
Every day, a singing
a sign given
against the slow alarm
of life not fully taken.

I hear the rumble of hooves let go
ringing inside the earth
the unearthing
of a life.

In the Open (1998)

Blue Place
for Eva, Jane and Grace

Last beach flowers: the color of asters, old bruised heart
suddenly out on a stalk blooming…
Light is always the first to know
as if the condition of the world
rested on each morning eyelid, dawn slowly spinning
out of view. So what's left for us
here by the edge of the sea where sails clog
what looks like the horizon.

Sunrise has rolled back in to the pink glow
of the head of the globe   What did we know?
We didn't know the words
and was there music   another land?
Countries listed off the map   beaches sandpapered
the air and the sea deep-lunged at us
across the tearing edges   Oh forgetful sun
moon and stars   out and shining
bareheaded in weather like this. It couldn't be
time to wake up: head bent with the weight
of startled voices   listening
to the end of dreaming and fighting to be heard.
Memory will not follow
tickle us or age   Only the enormous
accuracy of silence will imprint
our past   a soundless kiss on the lips   goodbye.

My hands fall easily into the hands of women
who stay each other   arms and whole bodies of tenderness
pass into this future with the aroma of suicide
salt in the air   in our mouths.
We move out from the blue
place   this palpable hurt on earth.
The sense of it: pain
but not blindness. No.

Dream: Women's Action

We have been seen. We are important or perhaps we are in the important area where the central ones are being transported. We are added to the bus and taken to the institutional building with the other women. The side opens. It looks like one of the truck entrances to the Pentagon. Isn't there a subway under here? Whose cars are those in the parking lot? This is a border. Are we near Canada, the woods thick on the horizon. Vermont, upstate New York, Canada. That's it. I

Inside, I am relieved it is a hospital, not a prison. I can breathe, then remember hospital means our bodies are under suspicion. My relief is only as long as my next breath. There is the silent comfort of the others. We have beds in the same large corner room. I am a little comforted. I lie down and promise not to touch my feet to the floor. This is the first rule I've heard.

I have a doctor who is called mine. I am thinking he will not hurt me. He doesn't look as if it's his fault he's here. I am forgiving him, and I turn on my stomach. He climbs on top of me and lies perfectly still. I sink under his weight without a sound. You might not know I am there, under him, his out- line so perfectly traces mine. Somehow, his body has been fed the information, the x-rays, and he has adapted the contours of his body to fit my bones. He is becoming a shadow of me. I am there and he is not. He wears light poplin and I am sheeted white. I am thinking of what the others will say, but I can't see them, I am so deep in my mattress. Quite suddenly, we are all up, hastened to inspect our quarters. There are large open windows. I know I can escape, the roof an easy drop. At the same moment, I realize no bars are needed. Every thought of escape is reversing itself into the destruction of our connectedness. They have turned the power of dreaming against us. I know I cannot live without my imagination.

My mother's brother enters and I remember he worked for Eisenhower before he opened his head on a stone wall deep in the Virginia woods. He looks down as if charged with a difficult duty. He is dressed in pale browns and looks soft. He announces in a quiet voice that he's made a mistake. There are eleven of us and only five may survive. There can be poison in the food at unannounced intervals. It doesn't matter which six go. In fact, we can choose.
Pistols may be given on request, one chamber loaded, and supervision.

My uncle says he's sorry, but it can't be helped. I scream No, striking at his face and chest, my arms aching from the blows. He does not try to protect himself, some acknowledgment of the injustice I think, then realize my blows leave no new marks. I see only the scar he carries from boyhood darkening in a diagonal along his cheek, the place where his fears bind, quickly sealing the cut: a boy, a bottle, a rocky beach and the glass through his cheek. The scar would be the premonition of his death: falling forward onto the stone wall as he looked for the short cut to town in the blizzard. He sought his wife and young daughter who had moved soon after he began slitting the tires. He cut in a diagonal along the smooth inside of the studded snow tires, his pulse beating hard in his hands and feet, the whiskey heat.

He found no way past the stone wall.

I look deeply into his face and know I have learned the same ways: how to drink and drive off the ones I love. I know how to make a wall my death. This is the closest we will get, he and I, this breath of loss between us. I reach for the women. He has given me valuable information, no protection.

Hawk

I

Your eyes on a moving target:
perhaps a mouse, muted brown near
the roots of the pale lined grasses.

Diving: eyes red as Mars
depth-charge the air.
Feet lace, cage the swirling fur.

I know you never lie— there is no place
safe from your constant curiosity.
You are all intention,

while outside your field of sight—
denial, the form you inherited as focus;
the form your wings take daily

to resist and funnel the wind.
You are the only one who attacks
in flight. Nothing escapes you.

II

And today, the accidental—
something without direction
like hope or chance— your life turned perfect

by uncritical surprise. Here you are—
chest up, road under open wings. Eyes shine,
red pearls over the heart, on gray and brown feathers.

Somehow you have landed here—
faultless on the ordinary pavement.
No one has touched you.

What a vision it must've been!
Spitfire, your eyes

rolled around the bone-hard world

of your skull and into the atmosphere.
Brilliant and small, you wore your pride—
dangling, busted, home.

Deadly Weapon
for Leslie, Rosa & Margaret who were there, 1981
and in memory of Charlie Howard, gay man murdered in Bangor, 1984

We came home to the stranger:
Scarsdale. The move to the city
still rattling at our backs, even our shadows ran
thin as threads, then wide as plates.
We blinked at the walls, their whiteness,
and moved furniture into comforting positions.
This night, we drove with country
determination— two women in a car
no one could see under the flowing sheet of rain.
Unused to locks, we lost
both sets of keys and had to break in,
then laughed, got out the smoke
and curled tight on the bed. Hot wind
blew hissing through the screen,
open window.

I lay naked on top of the sheets,
the green comforter slipped again
to the floor and your remaining clothing.
you turned the pages of your magazine—
lazily licking your fingers,
toking on the joint and gently slapping
the pages. "Making the scene
with a magazine," I leaned on your turning
arm and fell back, liking to be fed
tokes in a continuum. The dog pressed his chest
against the cardboard boxes collapsing
the sides, straining to get to the window, his nose
pointing to the open screen.
"Come here, Lou, out of the boxes."
The buzzer rang. We scowled at each other
and as you pulled on your jeans, you asked the door,
"Who is it?" The pounding, fisted, began a loud,
dull hammer over the rain.

Sweatpants by the bed, I slip
them on, turn for a shirt, a top, something.
Through the heat, it is the sound

of speed, a hissing splits the room. It feels just
like I've dreamt so often—dreaming of wars,
I am shot again and again, feel the burn
of bullets, the burn of being
alive is wondrous and strange.
I moan and drop by the bed, listen
to the crunch of sand on the floor by my shoes.
I see the short, yellow arrow,
stand up and hurl it at the window.
My hands do not have the power
of the triggered crossbow and the arrow
falls a dizzy, harmless end-over-end.
"You fuckhead, get the fuck out of here."
Scream at the waiting window
as you run between me and the opening,
snap off the light.

We move to the center room—
no windows here, fumble for the phone,
knock it to the floor. *What's the address*
remembering our apartment has no number,
but letters like signals. You collect the phone
in your hands, dial the police
through the operator. I am full of violence
and hold my thigh tightly, both hands,
wide as nets, look down, feel the blood
hot and sticky. Squeeze tighter. They ask,
"Is anyone wounded?" "No, no, Yes, yes
one of has been hit." Hang up. "They're coming."
"Who cares, I wish I had a gun to blast
the window, blow his face off."
The dog presses to my knees
under the table and you lean close,
"we've both been wounded."

You call Rosa and Margaret, call to say
what? "Something terrible has happened."
and you make the words work with your tears.
"We need you to come,
Yes, now. We're
all right. We need you." Hang up.
We look at each other, now we are seeing
in the dark, our chairs click

against each other, old bones, close,
chosen. We cannot touch and our bodies
have put on the weighted coat, the lie.
We have already moved to the inner lining
in the center of the apartment where we can't be
seen. We breathe together, rattling the mix
of hate and fear, blood in the air
and nested somewhere safe outside.
This is what the arrow wanted—
to strike us apart. The blue lights
flash at the edges of the shades
as we take each other's hands appearing
and disappearing before our eyes.

Two detectives question us. Six policemen stand around
the front room, arms moving, radios loud.
They are angry and talk to each other, unbelieving.
"In Scarsdale, who'd shoot two girls in Scarsdale?
With a crossbow? That's a long-range, deadly weapon."
You are the girl visiting. This they make up
themselves, unable to picture us in bed. We said we were
both in the bedroom. The medic escorts me into the bathroom,
"to have a look." I hear them ask you if you turned down
any guys recently, in a bar, anything like that.
"Easy now, pull down your pants, so I can see."
His hands turn my leg. I am miles away, can't believe
this man is touching me. The last question,
"Do you have any enemies?"

The nurse shows me the examining room,
pulls back the curtain. "Just one of you
can come." Rosa is holding you
knowing to touch. The curtain closes. Margaret
takes my hands. I see the nurse's calves
and white shoes leave. "Let yourself cry," Margaret tells me,
"I know how strong you are. You don't have to be
strong now." I hear my mother speaking
as she puts her arms around my neck—
one day in her dying she broke
and pulled me close, cried against my chest,
I can't be strong all the time.
Just once. I let the shot come up, a hailstone
in my throat. The nurse returns,

"What's the matter honey?
It's all over now."

No one can come with me
to be x-rayed— and it is the x-ray technician
who suggests I have been shot by Westchester's own
Dart Man. "I don't think they ever caught him.
The publicity died down, what with Son of Sam.
I never heard anymore." He pins me
in position, hip hard against the machine, drapes the gray
radiation shield across the top of my body.
I turn my face as he enters his protected booth.

I haven't been in a hospital
since I kissed my dead mother's forehead
goodbye in May. She had wanted
radiation. And it was her doctor, a young
man, who told her it would help.
Somehow, she believed him— like no other.
I've lost all modesty, she said and gave herself
to the cure, injections of platinum that searched
and searched her veins for a way
out. This most precious metal, white
gold, shone in her veins
like belief.

A man ran from our window
leaving his imprint in the mud—
the footprints filled with water, the definition
slurred as the ground gave way.
He is the one who saw
us, did not deny his vision, picked up
the closest weapon, aimed and fired.
There have been others, more
usual. My mother worked to keep
us apart, speaking to you
only when I was in the room,
when she felt she had to, that last Christmas
at home. Alone for a moment, she would always ask
you the same question: *When are you leaving,
what bus, what train, when did you say
you were going?* She refused to enter any house
we shared and when we thought she would

we moved all the furniture of her imagination
for her— the extra bed, the live example of our
separateness. So she stood at the door,
This isn't as bad as I thought and we knew
we had imagined well— taken on her mask
for our own and forced her to bless our lie.
There was nothing right for her
about you. When she died, you were the first
to ask, "When are you coming home?"

September 1981-87

Sparks Street

Mother, all your relatives are dead,
the ones we had to memorize
staring down the stories
and plates of glass, the dinners
we took to heart and slept with.
My head creased the pillows
and wore the perfunctory blue
of your goodnight kiss.

The dead still wait, dog
the doors, whites of the eyes
rolled up like a sleeve of moon
hanging in the atmosphere.
This is called memory
when the live ones leave,
grow out through the latches
and hold onto the keys.

Loose with banging, heavy
with inside fury, the house
was sold. The stories stayed in our heads, sure as winter
and the late, ungiving March wind.
Our eyes smarted in the cold.

My hands set like carved attachments
on the arms of the chair.
My mind blinking on and off,
I kept being
reminded of motion, struck
like a match, yes!
I could not for the life of me move
but sat and sat in the same chair
inside this, my last house, my home.

Family Tree

The brothers of both generations had a violence in common
as if creating pain was genius,
the pride of the family— a moron
couldn't have done better than Tom,
the eldest and first to roost
at the quick of his quick, caged brain.

He held his sister at bay with an attack
dog— just held the dog back from making strings
of her vocal chords. Let the dog snap. So that
was the story of why my grandmother always wore
 a brooch at her throat… the scars like grosgrain ribbon
to my small hands that prodded and adored her,
her with the softest hanging plum of sun-
blue skin just back of her smiling, pointed chin.

George took a knife, armed in broad daylight, got his
sister screaming and stopped her, screaming.
Chased her right out the window and onto the roof,
never once told how it took imagination, though he knew it
as courage. Back inside, he had only to twirl the carving knife
handle in his hand. After all, he was the eldest and the stand-in,
what with father dying way upstairs. It was his duty
to do the carving, the red meat falling slowly
to the platter. *Pass your plate.* And she sat—
first on one hand, then the other—my mother,
keeping her plate in front of her,
bone-white, refusing daughter.

Cut Scenes
for David

Call your brother home
Slowly say the bones.

I wake in the night— blossom,
no leaf. I am falling, yes, this is
the random float of beauty, full
veins of color detached from the tree,
the air capable of all things.

I wake in the fullness
of my still untethered past, body
whirling on my bones   praying to be let down
on the ground where I can walk away.

I am not dreaming, run
to the trees around my house—
quick up to branches, bark
lined on my cheek. Inside, face
against storm windows, I watch
the blue-gray print of breath disappear,
open the awkward aluminum fame.
Huge flakes pour in. I smell the cold's large holes
in the room—my hunger for raw elements
meeting the hunger of the cold.

I have sought the structure of the house—
studied blue in the foundation,
warm in the wood, the bright string of rooms—
to bury the sounds of humiliation,
quiet fire at the end of the corridor.

The doors change rooms, the windows
give on the same world: this we
that choked, entangled: mother/father
dying for a long time,
and two last ones, afloat in the nightmare we,
learning to fly by walking on the ground.

Negotiations
for my parents

1.

"I just wanted to tell you.
This is the day, he's going today."
I don't remember
asking anything but took in the trance-like
assuredness of her voice that morning.
"All right," accepting it like breath
and joined her in the aloneness...
even as I hated the telephone
in my hand, voice in my throat
and distance closing.

I touched the hot cold
let my father   dying
in close   ears open   hearing
nothing more from him

It was as she wanted
and I could only guess
he too wanted.
The intensity
of her voice holding
all the proprietary calm
and fear of her solo watch
meeting the raw
truth of it. She was ready
to give him over
even as she counted,
heart beating in the stone-lined well,
the moments alive before her.
No fear allayed, she refused
to negotiate beyond
what was essential.

Later telling me she thought
it was odd, when he packed
all his clothes for just a month
in the country, adding, "I didn't say

anything." She didn't feel
the air leaving his lungs and
not coming back, not then.
Or the tightness
of his chest and shoulders
as he felt all his suits
and shoes slowly filling
with strangers
and walking away

2.

What strikes me now is
the weight behind the few words—
"I knew he was gone
when he hit the floor."
"What happened?"
"He fell out of bed."

She was in the room
in the chair I had struggled
to speak from weeks before
as I sat trying to tell my father
news of my life
and the desires I had,
going back to school.
And not knowing how to tell
him the clear facts of my life—
how much I loved him
and counted on him, the source
and foundation of sanity,
gentleness, hope I had been able
to hold—It was so simple.
I wanted to echo his greeting of the world,
but I wasn't as good,
prone to prideful resistance and fear.
I didn't hide and I didn't speak,
the desire alive, the wordlessness
still and large—his sweet, interested face
craning forward, small breath
deepened by the line of oxygen
piped from the portable tanks.

His own words had to be short,
his breath couldn't carry them,
so the words must have
started to accumulate
then fallen
like stones in a crumbling well—
a few more falling each day
loosening the earth on the way down
until the depth of desire
could not be measured nor
the thousand expressions of it—
but the stones became the love
of holding the words inside
until they are just
the right ones
and match the conditions
perfectly—even the changing
and laughing, that kind of fluidity
and grace—

so when he fell,
he weighed every word
and then toppled, stone falling
before the open mouth of water.

He fell beside my mother,
his witness, who had heard it all
before, but jumped up from the
listening chair, quick crouch,
alight in all the sounds
this body can utter.

Q.E. II Bermuda to New York, 1956

We are berthed in Hamilton Harbor
ready to cast off. My eyes just over
the first rail, white pleats and dark trousers
to both sides. Boxed flowers
and yellow envelopes come up the plank
from men in blue suits and caps.
People throw flowers at the ship
I like this. Then I see we throw something else—
it's money. I dig for pennies.
Kids from there don't wear tops
and dive for money. Pennies
out of the water, fists high
each time he salutes me.
He tucks his head and goes under.
The engines start, coins
still shiny in the air.
Water churns white and I see the pink
of his mouth opening.
The wake covers his face.
Someone throws a life-saving ring.
He gets on, limbs trailing
in the water. They do not scold him
but lay him down, empty his pockets.
Pennies pool around his waist,
his arms and legs spill across the dock.
His eyes closing, some coins
silver by his head.

He doesn't move.
People surround him.
My mother leans out to see.
How come he's not moving?
Something tells me he's not ok.
Did the money do it?

Natural Enemies

I

Thanksgiving, a family gathers
to eat together. It is country,
by the sea— room enough
to run outside after the meal,
the air sharp, breath short, hot as the moments held inside.

We shake hands around the room,
the extras stand, look down
at my ruffled hair which never stays
but runs like loose shiny film
around the room. My cousins come downstairs.
I am told they have been waiting
all day to see me. The eldest catches
me with his first glance, hair
switches across my eyes.

His bulk fills the stairs, his hands
flash in front of him, come down the railing.
His hands take my hands, fling me out into the room,
a hearty laugh. This is what they will call *darling*.
I must hold on to these hands. The room whirls
around me. I am spinning away into the air.
It is the beginning of the anaesthesia.
This is supposed to be what I love.
Let me down I am praying
with my separated hands.
Let me down to the ground.

His mother laughs and tells the room
how well we get along, *and over twelve years between them.*
He is their size but I do not think
he is a grown-up. His hands take my face, touch
my bones, *How beautiful you will be.* I pray with separated
eyes for ugliness, for not seeing, for not looking
in the same direction— anything not to see as he does.
His largest hand covers my head, my blond hair thins
under it. His smallest, fastest hand runs between my legs.

I fold up and wing my way away
wishing my blond hair feathered gray and brown,
my body the speed of a bird.
I move to the light, my pale yellow
changing afternoon on the bed of his room.
My legs feel like fists as I make my way
down the stairs. They are having another
round of drinks. I grab my jacket and run
outside to the younger ones whose guns I easily pick up,
the death of imagination and say nothing
really happened.

The tablecloth hems us loosely in,
skirts our knees. These are my cousins, the hated
pale blond dogs and the missing
middle brother who has run away.
This I understand as I face my own
family, scattered, salt and pepper, along the white skirt
of linen. I have been told which chair has been stolen
from which relative's house but I like the new paint on them,
feel myself in the bright shell of hiding, sink
into the colors, the rugs, the paintings. I know how
to get away, steal myself from my own body and slip
out into the light. My family is not there. Not one of them
stays with me. I laugh out loud. They call it
joining in. We are having a feast.

    II

If the boys make fun
of me, I will be a monkey
and my lightness will take me
to the smallest, high tip of the tree.
Here I have feet like hands and hands like feet—
I can pull my own images out of the air
and drop theirs like bombs to the ground. I am lighter
than air. The ground is fear to me.
From up here, I'm just a shade
on the shadow of a tree.

When I am down, my legs pinned,
I roar inside, a lioness

with my claws. It is years later,
this image, the others who have accompanied me
begin their animal walk. I must speak with them
before we are told we are natural enemies.

I will start with you, mother. I have seen you as bird
and lioness too. Bird of prey, eagle, peacock
and battered, winged creature—the weight of your unmet
grace heavy in your broken-boned wings. Then angry,
you enter as cat, your huge paws ripping the grass
as you skim the dry ground. There is dust and the yellow
rush of power. Ears back, you have stopped listening
and attack. You want me to run beside you.

You are an animal who would kill. I have seen your iron
anger, flawless in the heat. There were never any marks,
so it became a question of belief. Trust was a filthy word
to you. A lioness will eat her own legs,
so the cubs can nurse. This is the kind of nurturing
you roared at me. Necessity is ugly, raw and true.

Now Elizabeth, it is you, mourning dove,
I've always felt closest to you.
One day you stood, the next you flew.
You are a seed I caught on the wind accidentally.
My mother told me finally, *you did have an older
sister*, after days and weeks of unconscious pestering.
I asked and asked for an older sister
not knowing you had already come and gone.

A tender cat appears, a mother you knew and I must
too, to see her. She lifts you by your loose-skinned
neck, your heavy head, shoulders you and carries the cloud-
blue eyes to a soft place among the rocks, the other graves
come real. She knew you would be coming here and asked only
that you not be marked, you who were always marked.
Your death, still. Head of wet brown curls, I heard you whispered
from the first, your loyalty as you travelled, always
beside her, hand in hand. Your passing, a clear signal
pressed, palm to palm, *I love you.*

Flowing Out, Away

I remember everything
by myself. Nights
the lights turn up loud
like music. The wicker chair
becomes the one who feels
no love and shines hard
through the white paint.
I converse with it softly   undoing
the weave of hard grasses, the stubbed brass
feet. I am crying for this
formality—these objects
bursting threads in my mind.

May 14, 1980

in memory, Clare Haskins Gates

You gestured *Up*, the morning here for you at last
and busied your body with putting out your fever's fire,
found coals fit for one more day. Making the bed around your body
I make my words as I go, turn in speechless corners; your piece
of the conversation, a clear blue glassy look, sky between us, separation.
You said, *We're going home.* The nurse read deeper into the paper.

Death slipped between us, tactile, all-of-a-piece
and pulsed my life-dray leaves on fire.
One-sided touch, my hands burn in the air, last
to let go, falling in the wax light of the room. Your face, a paper-
thin mute w rapping. You, too, are outside the body—
no healing this permanent wound of separation.

The lightning sky opens the dark in pieces,
desperate to find itself, the ground, the body
that could no longer hold the familiar, willful fire
lining your face, now crackles, explosive, outside the last
night's breathing. Will this be what I remember, lighting scrawls on blackpaper
or is this escaping from you, the rain, the lightning all-separating?

Black and white, nothing could be clearer, the body
is a mere house and cold at that, separated
from the rest of us here beside you, your last papers.
We bury ourselves in the tasks at hand, the endless pieces
that must relocate into another kind of lasting
or do we give up and throw the words wasted in the fire?

Who are we now? My cheekbones are yours, firing
red and pushing hard under my skin. The embarrassed daughter lasts
to admire the flickering structures of bone embodying
the likeness. Never the same nor now in separation,
my skin still burns easy as paper—
while you, you drove your anger in your heart, in pieces.

I scan the sky, flagged with fire-
boned fingers and let the center go, oh last
word or first to know. I am fresh as blank paper
and say simply: *Go.* Make the separation,

go from us all. I sit now, empty, with the body
and know it is not you. Peace.

We write the obituary for the papers and separate
the body from the facts of your life. Burn the body in the fire.
What lasts is the world in pieces.

Calm Exteriors

for Joan

Calm exteriors betray themselves
like my father busy dying,
like my face driving the air
dull around me. The buds pellet down,
stone the storm windows, still on
as we stare outside the frigid
core of my father's air-
conditioned room. Our dumb skins crawl
and wait, the climate breathless, hot or cold.
This is July. It will never rain.

Hoping the hoarse breathing had stilled, I walked
outside on the wet grass, the green watery
lawn soothing my feet and fell weeping
out of earshot, under the apple tree.
I assumed I was alone, that my voice
thinned off and did not pass through the walls
but the walls were membranes and the dying
senses flash out gloriously one by one.
So it must have been: my father's habit
of reading, bathrobed, through the night
brought me into his pages. *Are you all*
right? and the man without breath
or speech came to ask me ever so kindly
back to the house, back to the trusting
walls where osmosis deepened
the summer night rain.

One to One, for Leslie

I

Our love began 50's style in a Ford Galaxy—
long wide seats and traditional love knot,
legs and arms tangled listening
to the other's news. Every night, the first
summer, slick sides to everything, melons
cantaloupe and honeydew. July's exploding
fireworks reached all the way through August.

You drew my hunger slowly out,
your golden paws expert, letting
tenderness weight the air
to bring my asking to a close.
You pinned my wrists in cool pillows
and rolled over me in a wave.

II

We passed The Country View late that fall—
it was there the engine rattled, backfired and blew.
The nearest farmhouse, Milton's Hilton, New Yorkers
moved north: The Wife sat jeering The Game
from her chair, the year the Sox came so close.
We lurked in the kitchen el while he
got permission to drive us home, twenty miles
to South Brooksville. You girls
don't want to be out in this, the first snow.
We'll see the Ford's off the road, don't want her
catching it with the side of the plow. Nice-looking
body, she's worth something sure. The old tortoise
shell grown slow in winter. We
heaved into bed, posts centered in that cold,
third-floor room and heaped up new walls
with the old quilts, let frost come
white onto the inside panes. Slow paling
of our bodies, just a form of hiding,
when winter presses the blood further in.

III

Confusion burrows in and marks the food, bed,
music, the personalities we keep
whose changing touch and mouthing silences
iron moods in and out of our clothes.
This year, the spring lets us out
into the City and we are on the run,
our shadows the first to feel
the sorrow ahead. I do not look
for magnet sameness
but seek the ragged river, flashing forks
where we diverge—
not name it Plattsburgh on the map
but how to reach through spooling falls,
from inside walls, what landscape stops the eye,
mica chips embedded in your gaze.

IV

You're driving out Long Island tonight.
This is where you grew up, where the orchards
were, a few isolated oaks and new brick
schools. Your mother's bottles
leaked poison to the street—
slamming windows and pulling shades, you
whispered fiercely at the neighbors from the cracks,
Get out of here if you know what's good for you.

The bitter gossip hushed a quiet self-hatred.
You poured and poured the golden braids of Scotch
down the drain and hid the new ones just delivered
to the front door. When the doorbell rang, you unsnapped
your mother's purse and paid. The nickels and lipstick
stuck with tobacco flakes. You wanted
no more money in your hands.

You are driving out Long Island tonight
making no waves, while inside, the child
says, *Take me with you, take me away—*
Let me come home and find a body I can call mine.

Conversation with the Body

My sex opens like a fan: thigh, thigh, thigh—
bones like rays elongate; the breath

lights the fingers, the palms blink open
and listen to the air. The body swims
after it—out of breath.

No one is here beside me—
just the suspended questions
that shine—asking
how to touch. I hear
answering all along my spine. Stars
flex in the high hum of the dark.

I've broken out of expectations,
don't look for a lover
and yet, at first, inspect everything—
grumpy, kicking the newly empty
boxes around the room without
doors where the unexpected
moves ahead of me.

I'm talking now—taking my body
for a ride in the atmosphere   having
volcanoed out, spit rock from my stone lap,
violet-red pebble rage.
I inhabit the soft-hair surfaces,
hot-pulse the air
marking space like the tiger
in the tiger coat.

What is it, my hands could
almost touch? Open, unready,
not lost or waiting... this
body and no other.

Wild Blue

My rich cloudbank with the many blue backs—
boneless, beautiful disaster—so tired of this
present, the purple dust I face,
constant in my eyes; sunsets and proud moonlight
I am always covering. What's inside,
oh wild blue confusion: moisture clinging
to the dust of the universe. I come from

everywhere with no place to go.
How to feel welcome next to the bright, hard
metal of stars. My absence is considered
a miracle on cloudless days. I rest
dissipated, fallen into snow, condensation
to the garden stirring out of the ground.

Anything is possible.
Even secrets, hinged like dark blue shells
grown under the coldest waters,
release: spin fire to the surface,
break skyward and open to the world:
wild blue telling all in calm freefall
before disappearing like skywriting.

Triptych

for Ron King, Lynnsey Carroll and Tracy Sampson

I: RON

Charlie said he wanted to die
and Dell and I were the ones,
of course, who were going to
help him do it. You know Dell—
Charlie's ex, most recent
ex. Well, the exes were
elected, me and Dell.
No one in the family
was going to do it, and Charlie said
he was ready this time. You know last
summer he almost died, we had
bedside vigils, the whole bit, then he
felt better and went to Florida
for the winter. Stayed in the trailer park
with his brother, Dirk. Yeah, that's right,
same time that I broke my leg,
6 foot 4 inch faggot in a cast
and Charlie was feeling okay then,
so he rode me all around the fucking
trailer park on that giant
tricycle. What a picture.
Anyway, Charlie was ready to die,
so we did all the preparation,
read the book by what's-his-name—
Humphrey—got the pills.
Everyone knew, the family
was supportive. None of them
wanted to *be there*, but they were ready
because Charlie was ready. They all
came and said their goodbyes, so Dell and I
go over to Charlie's house on Saturday night
with all the stuff expecting to wake up
with Charlie dead. All three of us—

Dell, Charlie and me—had read the instructions
five or six times each, of course, but we
were nervous as shit. The pills are supposed to

work better with alcohol, so I had some Scotch ready.
He wouldn't take it.
He was adamant, he wouldn't touch the
stuff, said it had been hard enough
to get sober and stay sober. He insisted
on water, even though I begged
him. I told him it didn't make any
difference. He wanted to go out
sober though. So I gave him the pills—
with water. He had stopped eating—was just
taking fluids, so swallowing the pills
wasn't easy. He took every
one of those suckers, ten of them,
drank them down one at a time, thanked me
and lay down. We waited, set beside him
for two hours, then went in the other
room. Dell lay down and I set the clock,
just in case, but I couldn't sleep at all,
of course. Got up at 2, went and checked
on him, he was still breathing,
the fucker, so I went back
and told Dell, who was wide awake,
that he was still alive.

I got up again at a little after 3, looked
in and his chest wasn't moving, I was sure
this was it. I woke
Dell up, told him Charlie had
stopped breathing. I'd promised
to call Charlie's brother, Dirk,
yeah, the straight one, the one closest
to him, and there was Sue, a really close
woman friend from the program. She
said she wanted to know when he died. So I called
Dirk's and got his machine. Couldn't deal
with that so I hung up. I got
Sue and she thanked me. I sat down and had
a cigarette when Dell came back in the room,
and said he had closed Charlie's eyes.
I shrieked, "You what? His eyes weren't
open when I was in there." We ran
back and took his pulse. It was
going. The fucker was still alive

and I swear he wasn't breathing when I was
in there. We didn't know what to do, felt
guilty as hell that we'd failed him,
went into the kitchen to talk and have more
cigarettes. We found a garbage bag
in there and decided to try
and smother him. So there's Dell and me,
scared to death, creeping up either side
of the bed, ready to pull this bag
over his head and hold him down if he
struggles. What a picture we must've made.
We're just ready to slip the bag
over his head and his eyes pop open.
We just couldn't do it: pull a bag over a man's
head with him staring at us. We left
the room and talked and talked,
harangued over not doing
our job, about failing him,
and finally, thank God, we realized we'd done
enough, that it wasn't our job to do
anymore. It was his job and he'd have to
do it himself if he wanted to die.
I had to call Sue back
and tell her Charlie was not dead.

I am exhausted waiting
for Charlie to die. I feel this
incredible weight but I just can't
do anything more about it. This week
I realized the fucker repeated
the same thing that happened
over and over in our relationship. I'd get
all the information, try to do it
all for him, and he wouldn't be ready.
Then when I'd just about given up, he'd go
do it himself. Well, this is something
I can't do for him. I love him
but he's just going to have to die himself.

II: CATHY

Well, since I became a lesbian…
You mean last week, Lynnsey
interrupts laughing. We all
laugh, glad to, after Charlie's
funeral, laughing at how much is
possible after all. Cathy
leaps ahead headlong. Yeah, well,
it's been three weeks, actually.
I'll tell you my life has really
changed. Being HIV Positive
is nothing compared to this.
Course I can't stop talking
about it and you know, not
everyone wants to hear about it either.
This gets a big laugh from back and front
seat. And you people, well my God,
I've got four dykes
right here in one car.
I have to hear all
about how you met, you know,
how you got together.
I don't know what I'm doing.
I've been talking
about it in my meetings
but they think they've heard enough,
what with me being HIV Positive
and all, they don't want to hear
about my being a lesbian too.
They've been through Harry,
my ex-lover dying from AIDS, two
years now it's been, and my ex-
husband and his being positive
now too. You just don't know.
Now my ex-husband, he's not
threatened or anything. And my support
group in Bangor, they're good,
and of course, the gay/lesbian meeting, but
I need to talk about this a lot
and my regular AA home group
in Bangor, well, one of them,
I thought she was my friend, she says

to me, Cathy, it's too much. We're just
here to talk about problems of alcoholism.
We heard all about Harry's IV drug use
and your HIV, but this is too much.
They think it's a tragedy. She doesn't
understand that I'm happier
than I've ever been in my whole entire
life. After thirty-two years, I am finally
in the right place at the right time.
I'm fine. I don't want to drink. Another thing,
a lot of straight people, they think
if I've said it out loud
once, I should be done.
They don't understand this being
a lesbian changes everything in my life.
Everything. I barely know
what to say anymore, I want
to tell everyone of course, my family
and my old friends from school but I can
see from the reaction at meetings
that I'm going to have to be more
selective, pick and choose who
I talk to because I don't need
any shit about this—like I said,
this is the best thing that ever
happened to me. And it *is* related
to my sobriety, goddammit. If I wasn't
sober, I wouldn't know how to think
over anything. I was hiding
all the time, drowning in booze.
Now I'm making some real
choices and I'm pleased as punch
about it. I listen to everyone
else tell about their relationships—
wives, weddings, bosses, you name it.
I don't complain. I get something
out of it. Well, they should
be able to, too. It's crazy.
They haven't heard near
enough from me. Why
shouldn't I be able to talk
about being lesbian?
It's good for 'em

to see there are other ways
of loving. My ex-husband
he understands no problem.
He's one of my best friends. He
called in the middle of the night, the other
night. He was freaking out—
not about me—about being Positive
now too—and he couldn't think of anyone
else to call. What guy can he call?
Guys don't talk to guys, at least not straight
ones. He doesn't have any supports yet, it's so new.
He kept apologizing for calling
but he really didn't know
who else to call. So I talked with him
for awhile, calmed him down
some, told him it was a big
adjustment and he didn't have to
do it alone, that there were
all kinds of supports now—thanks
to you Lynnsey and you Tracy.
I told him how 2 lesbians started
Down East AIDS Network and got the guys,
the political ones, working too,
and how you worked with the state
agencies and got grants, how you
started it all in your own home,
had the office on the stairs
and how D.E.A.N. had a big office now
and two paid positions, all because
you just fucking did it, organized
it right here in Down East Maine.
I told him how it was for lovers
and family members, for straight
people too. I gave him
the whole nine yards. I told him he can go
to the support group like I did—
get mad, talk about it,
let it out, and eventually he'd
maybe get to where he could accept
it and get on with his
life. You know it makes you
think. I didn't paint too rosy
a picture for him. The anger, grief

and pain all came back, after all
we're only human. But he can
find people, good ones
he can trust, then
get on with it, the way
I have. Anyway, he said he felt
a lot better and thanked me
and said 'God bless 'em' about
you Lynnsey and you Tracy.
He'll be all right. I know
he will. But I got to meet
some women. I need to hear
all I can to get ready.
Now Lynnsey and Tracy, you met here in Maine,
Right? So there's hope for me.
I need to hear all
about it, everything. Then
we can move on to you, Bea,
and you, Roz. You're from another
country. I'd like to hear about that.
Hell, maybe I should come down
to New York and meet some women.

III. HOMELESS

Morning sun outside D'Agostino's, a young man bends,
crooked towards a parked car, heavy brown
raincoat, denim jeans and white shirt.
Smooth face, dark brown beard, hair shiny
in gentle curls away from his face.
His skin: translucent, taut across the bones
in his face, pink cheeks. His brow: a dome
over liquid brown eyes, deep-set under dark
eyebrows, long lashes. In one hand, he clasps
a sheaf of papers, his fingers curled.
He holds the papers up, shield at shoulder-height.
"Excuse me, I need help."
I walk towards him, he's not
threatening. I see his physical
weakness. "I was in a hotel," he says, "I was robbed,
they beat me up," I see the bruise on the side of his face
and look again into his eyes. I stop,

rest my bags at my feet. "It's dangerous
now," he continues, "It's no good anymore. They ruined it.
The addicts. They steal everything. They stole
my money, my medicine, my AZT. They sell it on the street."
His eyes start to brim, "I get my check this week, see"
he holds the papers towards me, "see, there's my ID,
here's my papers. See, it's me." The tiny square
snapshot shows a large head, shorn.
I tell him to hold on to his
papers. I don't need to see
them. I ask if he's been to GMHC. "Yeah,
they got me a place, at the AIDS Hospice."
he gestures down the street towards Christopher.
"GMHC only takes people under $5000, my checks put me over,
but they got me a referral to the hospice." He stops,
eyes brimming again, "I'm sorry," he looks down, shifts
his weight, stumbles in the space between the car
and the curb, touches my arm inadvertently, draws back
fast, "I didn't mean to touch you, I'm
sorry." I steady his elbow. "I'm so tired,"
he leans against the brown coupe outside the French restaurant.
"What do you need?"
"I'm so ashamed, I hate asking
for anything. I ate out of a garbage can this morning.
I never did that before. I ate someone's leftover McDonald's."
"It's OK, you were hungry, you got some food."
He begins to cry, then stops, "I'm gay, my father."
"What's your name?" I ask. "What do you need?"
"I'm so ashamed for asking like this,
I just have to. I got to get to the McBurney Y,
they have a room for one night they said,
if I can get up there. I need to rest. I have lesions
on my legs," he pats his blue-jeaned thighs,
"they get infected, I got to clean them out, get
some peroxide." I know I have money
in my pocket, thirty dollars in the bank.
I reach in my pocket, pull out a ten-
dollar bill, direct him, "Go out to Hudson,
you know the park…"
"I need to sit down," he interrupts, "I'm so tired…"
"You know the benches, you can sit down and rest
on one of the benches down the street by the laundromat.
When you're ready, get a cab on 8th. It'll take you right up

to the Y." I have never given anyone
a ten-dollar bill on the street before.
"I can get your address and pay you back, I get my check next week."
"Forget it, go sit down, go to the Y, sleep, rest."
"I can't thank you enough. Bless you, thank you," he crosses Greenwich
towards Hudson. I turn, my hands barely able to grasp
the two bags of groceries, lift the weight,
carry them around the corner.
I turn, see the back of his
raincoat, the beautiful chestnut curls
over his collar.

Next week, I am headed to the bank
to deposit a check. I am celebrating,
Thank God! Down to my last two dollars.
Right outside the bank, I see him in his raincoat talking
with a young woman clearly on her way to work.
She is gesturing, "Go to the Center, the Gay/Lesbian
Center on West 13th St.," she is over-pronouncing
her words. He is repeating, "the Center, the Center"
as if he's never heard of it. I pass them
quickly, fury carrying me into the bank.
I make out a deposit slip, fill in
the date, bank account #, the deposit for $357,
sign my name. I decide to confront him
when I'm done, if he's still out there. *Remember me,*
I'll say. Lying son of a bitch, draining off women's
energy, lesbian energy like no one
ever dies from anything besides AIDS. Community,
my ass. How many gay men are nursing women
with breast cancer or anything else for that matter.
The Y. Goddam liar.
What happened to my ten dollars, you son of a bitch?
I pad quickly over to the express
deposit, put in my bank card,
check my balance: —$10.50. Shit, what happened?
I seal the envelope, pop it
in the slot, punch in the envelope number
and it drops safely in.
Get the deposit slip, $2 till tomorrow—$1
for milk, 65¢ for a cup in the morning, 35¢
for NEWSDAY, and by 3 the check will clear.
Minus $10.50, what happened?

Christ, who knows. At least I got
paid, I'll be OK.

Outside, the corner is empty, swept clear, a short
line to the ATM. *Remember me*
Maybe he wouldn't remember, maybe
he couldn't remember…
Why didn't he know The Center?
I begin to choke on my own breath
as I realize he may not remember.
AIDS in later stages.
Is he lying or not remembering?
Is he dying or running a scam
or both? Does he know the difference? Do I?
Do I need or deserve to know
because I gave him $10, because
I'm a lesbian who has seen too
much of this disease?
Anything could have happened.
We live in New York City.
I wanted it to be simple: cross
the street, go sit down, rest,
get the cab uptown, then sleep.

In the morning breakfast,
take a cab to the AIDS
hospice. Here he enters a place where
he will die. I want to know
I have finished. But he has not
arrived anywhere. I bumped into him,
the motion of his life down the street.
He showed me that it was the world,
not he himself alone who held
his body in his hands.

Arms of gold, red, brown and black

11/17/93, for Barbara

Audre prepared a nest for you, a warrior's
woven offering—weft facing outward, weave
laid bright over curling boughs—a strong, sheltered space,
rough as bark's protection,
flexible as sap gathered
tight in heart wood. Audre carried you
into New York City where you came to confer
on how best to mark her passing.

I saw Audre
in the elevator, head bound, riding
in full African dress and telling me—
I'll take care of this, *for Barbara.*
The doors closed and she ascended
with a small bow of recognition
towards what was needed at the time.

Bones bitten with loss,
you jumped in front of a cab to stop it.

I said, "Don't freeze to death,"
and you, "I *am* freezing to death."

And what could we do
together? Audre always asked, Audre the one
who slipped through the universe, shot heat
boldly from her center, fully, careful to touch
the crown of your head, and encircle
you, an African American lesbian—still standing,
more alone. She bore your weight
stood by, carefully marking
this time in shadow, the situation turning—the power
of loving clear. Taking on some
of what had passed between you, seeing more
clearly what would be asked for in the days ahead:

I was frightened for you
and let my bones lengthen into it.

Pond

for Eva

I loved you as if we had touched
the billowing air that spun our fresh-mown
thoughts: heady August, your amber eyes like rays.
Leonine, you watched me: deeply shaded and alone.
I loved the sparks of grass pale green and blonde,
flung wide as you rolled down the length of lawn.
We walked the steep, damp path to the pond,
divided the surface into lines on the face
of difference, the softening creases
around your joints, my large hope like the water between us.
Gray head tipped water-dark, I watched
you go and swam hard into acceptance
wanting exhaustion and a map for distance.
I loved you as if we had touched.

23rd Street Cineplex

Denis's eyes clear blue and bright,
his body a wand.
—How are you?— and I see
his pupils glare
—I'm in a rage. Everything,
just everything—
—What's going on?—
—I want to live—
The words flare, drop
on the sidewalk, then curl
in charcoal at our feet

I hold Denis tight in my gaze
as we ripple together
in the brutal spring tide
of fresh river scent.
I hold the daily forms of rupture
tenderly, new to the spider's
art, the web of spit
and long drop from center.

Is it his death or mine
standing beside us   camouflaged as one
waiting casually for another
as our bones point with murderous urban
accuracy to the theatre entrance.

Dream: Bay Foal
for Roz

I was given a beauty
wide sweet head
and I rubbed her right
between the eyes.
She pressed hard
against my palm. She adored
me. Soft gray eyelids, nostrils
of the same smoky flesh.
Velvet mouth and nose
whiskers.

She curled, all legs, in my lap
her hooves held high
in the air   dark horn
tips   from the rippling basket
of limbs she formed
in my arms: A love.

The muscles in her flanks
liquid as I stroked
and rubbed her down.
Her new bones turned easy
muscles gliding between
my fingers, almost fingers themselves,
the deep pleasure pushing back
the chords of power
under her beautiful brown
skin. This cannot keep
up   I thought   the first cold
to enter the dream.

Full gaze.
She turned her muscled neck
thick shiny chestnut
then nibbled   sucking, pulling
on all my fingers
in twos and threes.

To think I almost gave

the foal away
to play with a braid
of wind.

Praise for the A Train
for Electa

I sit down beside the song, the woman
singing straight ahead, her needles
at work crocheting shawl,
slow mountain rising across her lap.
Her voice makes me open, porous, hungry.
Not seeing but believing, I close my eyes,
the train filling in bright air,
longing safe in the shawl of comfort she is
stitching in and around us. We need her.
She doesn't care. We lean out into the tunnel,
bright sail before her song—rapt, loyal,
forgetting any danger. Sailing underground on steel wheels,
The blue "A", the signal of our naked happiness.
We lay down all our resistances,
surrender to the voice of a woman
becoming the song of our train.

Refuge

I

All day it snowed and we bore further into it—no visible progress, a hot core
of comfort in the warm car—hot feet, radio and you dozing off as I peered into
the unseeable spinning wind. Blizzard conditions. Next day, in the deep quiet
of the snow, we walked the road to the nature preserve, cut across the open
slope, the sky's crackling blue above us.

We waded through the deep surrounding
snow: my thighs burned in the cold soft parting
Hands hooked on my waistband
you pull me from behind: I turn easy
as a spool of lavender-shaded twine
in your hands, stand in the
enlarged silence as you secure expectation—
I want you here—
take off your coat and kneel to lay it down
in the fresh path my legs have made before you.

II

Looking up   your face changing fast
full of what you want
we have met in the shaking space
inside the snow globe   all desire
water around us   snow loose on the ground
ready to be shaken   to be touched
stripping the cover from the hot cold
quivering hillside   my skin hot
against the snow.

No cold or words between us
your hands know what they want   unzip my pants
enough to thread folded fingers
between my thighs   Heated soft, I sit quietly on your slowly
turning hand   receiving brushed bone-sensitive
jumping pulses   I hold your shoulders   raise up
my breasts seeing what they want against the cloth:

shirt buttons in your teeth   soft blue
cotton damp from your tongue   nipples seeking
the eyelet of your open mouth   the talking back:
get serious   don't let go   keep me shaking

your mouth the only hold on what I want
I fall back on my heels   want to stay
standing   want to let you
drive me crazy before wanting to
let you drive me there

III

We climb the crest of the hill to the summer
house   stand looking out at our abandoned
trail   sex angels in the now   bodies still warm and finding
new outlines in the sun   the whole porch, a sudden open prow,
wood warm to the touch   We say nothing
sun catching us still open to sex
but take it in: the whole porch facing south
minds ticking over everything we might want to do
in this freeing blue unusual air
I move back against the broad wall of the house
hot ribbed shingles under my palms
lancing eyes as this time you drop in front of me
open my loosened jeans and place your whole mouth
fast on my cunt   Head-back held   you are deep under now
calling for light as you begin to swim through me
My hands knead your jaw as I unmoor and go
Sun in your mouth
I am no longer any one fire

IV

We waded through the snow/ our bodies sudden, weighted against the infinite
cold/ sky ripped wide to hot sun/ throwing our bodies forward into the curve
of the hillside/ churning water down the iced cove/ salt gleaming on the
glacier's broken dark gold rocks/ shattered motion of sea further out/ I begin to
run by falling forward/ thighs burning as I part the snow/ jagged softness/
reach a shallow cradle in the slope and gaining/ you pull me back against your
vest/ wrap me in your coat/ *I want you right here!*/ Full mouth over-the-shoulder

kiss/ You peel down quickly/ your coat, a raft in the snow/ desire speeding
your efficiency/ I watch in studied patience to slow your every ardent move/
determined to break open all the space we need/ Coat lies peaceful, teasing,
smoothed over our tracks/ You fall forward even as you are pulling me down
by the belt loops/ *right now*/ on my knees.

V

This is the last winter the house will stand.
In the spring it will be destroyed.
Perhaps this is what the old woman meant
when she left the codicil to her will:
when I die, tear the house down,
burn what remains and leave
the land forever wild

Changing Places
for Jean

Who is this stranger?
She is lighter than the other
characters I keep and walks towards me.
Arms, a smile—I know you,
wordless, amused, then out loud,
"Tell me anything.
I haven't heard enough from you.
And I've been here."
She seems to have the laughter to prove it
—ragged, deep, changing places.

Let the din you were afraid had no place to go
but further in, out the sorrow head.
Flame stutterer has more to say.

Toll the bright echo.

Sorrow cup,
how well you hold the sun.
Pounding bass   glory's hay head.
Do not leave yourself alone.

Stranger cups my head in her hands.

Ten Minutes (2006)

Seeking Tenderness
for Matthew Shepard

I

Blood cake cowlick
Palms like kleenex
Brow cleaved open
Skull cocked hat.

Deaf to music
Shirt tails billow
Hard October
Birds won't land here.
Bright-seeing silent night.

II

Stories walk backwards
out of the split-rail lodgepole pine,
the deer fence where you hung,
limbs scorched, star-stung, rusty throated
no song:

Once Chastity hid her boyfriend Russell's bloody clothes,
the girlfriends helped make up alibis. They couldn't
decide what to do with Matthew's size 6,
black patent-leather shoes. The wallet
tossed empty on a night table,
the shoes gleamed in the trailer's corridor.
And what would Aaron say
if Kristen admitted she wanted to try them on?
She kept her mouth shut, chewed at the corners
(same as when she said, "they just wanted to beat him up
bad enough to teach him a lesson," talking later to 20/20)
but the black patent-leather shoes glistened,
strange and magnetic like a city, a place she'd never walked,
full of dark mirrors where she could look in
and one minute see the great night sky
and the next, laugh at their small distorted faces leaning over
to study the faggot's favorite shoes

trying to figure out whether to ditch them or not.

Someone said that Aaron, like a lot of people who talk alot,
had nothing to say, that his friends called him a shrimp,
just bullied him around, put him in a headlock and held him
there. "He wasn't the mean guy,"
one said, "he was just Aaron, the little guy."

When Doc, the limo driver from Doc's Class Act
pulled up in the 25' white Lincoln stretch
Matthew said, "I want you to know right now
I'm gay and we're going to a gay bar. Do you have a problem with that?"
And Doc threw back, "How are you paying?"
laughing as a friendship began. Shepard worried
about splurging on the trip to Fort Collins for an all-nighter
with his friends at Tornado and how badly he wanted to go
where he could dance and swing in another man's arms.
"He would tell you anything," Doc marveled
about his talks with his new customer.
Doc was friends with another set of regulars,
Aaron and Russell, and had given an apartment
he had in town rent-free to Aaron, Kristen
and their young son.

Now when Doc drives by that stretch of road
accelerating up the bluff a mile east of town,
he sings loud to the radio trying to block the voices
he hears in the wind crying "no-good faggot" and "please, please
don't kill me." Later, he can't help
replaying Matthew:
"If I could get two people who hate each other—
one straight, one gay—to be respectful of each other,
I would have done something good." This is the song
that keeps finding him and he cannot repeat.
He still feels for the two who killed,
so he drives the roads at all hours, slow
then fast, then steady, driving
whoever needs to get somewhere else for whatever reason.
He sits behind the wheel tapping out the hours
against the leather-encased rim,
the blue-dark empty sky in front of him.

"Russell's about the most American

kid you can get. He's a pizza-eating, beer-drinking,
fishing, hunting, work-on-your-car
type of kid—just regular," his landlady said.
Russell's mother, Cindy, was found frozen
1000' from a highway shortly after dawn in the new year.
She was wearing a shirt, jeans and a pink nylon jacket.
The bartender at the Buckhorn Bar had refused
to serve her saying she was too drunk already
and asked her to go stand by the window
to wait for her ride. What did she see?
The tail lights blurring or a big TV
coming closer like the one her husband pushed
her head through? She walked 4 miles that night.
Wind came and carved
her senses awake: too late, she knew
where she was headed, drove her legs
towards the line of hills, the cut of road ahead
until she couldn't face it anymore.
Jacket zipped high around her neck,
she stopped. Wind drove her down
to the hard pan where she lay in the shelter
of the Arctic cold.
Russell said his parents were dead.
a Taco-Bell co-worker said,
"I didn't even know he had them in town."

III

"Guess what?
I'm not gay and you
just got jacked."

Truck door shut,
Russell pulls out the .357-caliber magnum,
angles the butt of the handle
and begins.

The bicyclist who found Matthew Shepard
thought he was a scarecrow
until he saw the human hair.

Wall of wind

breaks the spine of words.

IV

Later, he will fly,
wrists still bound to the fence,
the wind in back of him
easily lifting him off his feet.
He will fly towards them
as they turn towards home
after a night on the town.

He will be like billowing
clouds that rake the plains
this time of year, change hour to hour, comb the grasses
silver, then red, keep coming.
He will fly, one of a flock of birds
that keeps darkening the sky as they pour
over the plains with the force of water.
He will be flying with grace and purpose
trying out all the angles learned by those
who have gone before:
how to fly while being dragged
through the hot dirt in Jasper,
Texas at the end of a rope
tied to the bumper of a pickup truck,
or how to sing through the eyes
like the two women lovers looking for a house,
gagged then bound back to back,
who took bullets to the head
in southeastern Oregon.
He will fly because he is hungry
for it, the beautiful mouth of the sky
taking in all he has to give, the tenderness
of beating wings all around him.

Dream: Inaugural 2000

Broad wingspan, one wing marred,
no sheath between feathers, open
slots of air altering the speed of flight.
I shout to mark the occasion,
the arrival and passing of this beauty, wings oaring space
then entering a glide.

The eagle wheels, heads towards us
in a full summer afternoon, golden light
in Central Park. We are gathered in many
casual ways. I see the bird growing huge
and fill with the happiness of the honor—
wings sweeping backwards, ready to land.
I am shouting with joy
Look, Look, the eagle is landing among us.
The sound of the bird touching earth is fierce
and I run to stand near, hear a sharp punctuation
inside the wind. Fire pins the bird against the empty bleachers,
walkways, now rivers spreading out
red among, between us.
I remember where I live, this country
the gold eyes saw.

2/16/03
for Grace & Bob

"They snuck by the French,
they did it without them,"
I crush the news into pellets
for morning's bitter vaccine.
We admit, as Grace said,
it's been a few very bad years
feeling the world
unreconstructable.
"We're dreamers, Bea, we're dreamers,"
not sadder, "we're dreaming."

In the afternoon, I read from the World War II novel
about fighting the passage of deepening sorrow in Warsaw,
fighting despair in the city where everything
had happened, fighting tiredness
of a kind that isn't about sleep—
The man escaped
Warsaw in an undertaker's pine box
smuggled out in a coma
remembering little after his bad leap across rooves,
slippery tiles, and his head-on collision with the fire escape,
keeling over, bloody forehead, through the window
into someone's cold sunny breakfast,
someone who knew how and where to push him
safely through:
across the hall, into the capable
hands of the pine box builder
who handled every size and shape
and gladly added this dangerous
one to his ongoing job,
fit him up and sent him on.
So he arrived into a forest
a small house
as if awakened from a dream
faces of care, concern.
He awoke
escaped but nowhere found—
as if from a dream.

To the Editor of "The Ellsworth American" (February 17, 1876)

Mr. Editor:—

In the first place, I object decidedly to the body of water
over which it is proposed to construct this bridge
being called "Sullivan River." It is not
in any sense such a body of water.
It is really a narrow passageway between two salt water bays
where on the flood tide the water from Frenchman Bay
rushes through with great velocity to fill a large salt water bay above;
then, on the ebb tide it rushes with almost equal velocity
to find its level in Frenchman Bay below.
It may be called Sullivan River; but that term, in my mind,
would mislead a person unacquainted with the facts, as to the waters,
the navigation of which it was proposed to obstruct by building a bridge.
So much for the fraud upon the public with which this matter starts out.

Now for the facts, as to the "slight inconvenience of going through a draw,"
I think it would be well, *always*, for a person who proposes to instruct
the public, that he should know *something*
of the *facts* bearing on the question.
—What are they in this case?
First, there are in the vicinity of 250 vessels passing through "Sullivan Falls,"
each way, every season, engaged in carrying to market
the lumber, wood, bark, piling, spars, railroad ties, granite, etc
shipped from the town of Franklin and points in Sullivan and Hancock.

These 250 vessels are obliged to have what is called a leading, or fair wind,
to make the passage of said falls going out;
such a wind is between the points S.W. and N.N.E.
going round to the Westward, and the passage can only be made
at high water slack, in the day time;
no such thing is ever attempted as passing them
at any other time of tide, or in the night.

The proposed site of the bridge is some three-fourths of a mile above the falls;
between the falls and this point, there is not one foot of safe anchorage for vessels.
Now as to the "slight inconvenience of going through a draw in said bridge"
to vessels coming *up through the falls.*
A vessel now coming into Sullivan, bound to Franklin, or any point in Hancock

above said falls, has, in case the tide is running out when she gets there,
merely to wait till the tide commences to run *up* through the falls;
then they can go right along about their business, nothing to hinder,
nothing to bother; often making the passage *up* through the falls,
against a head wind, or what in sea-going phrase, is called "beating through,"
and having such a strong fair tide, have no trouble in working up to our bay
    on the same tide.

In case of a strong, fair wind and a bridge draw as well to pass,
it would be with utmost risk that a vessel could come through at all.
Why? Because in the absence of any safe anchorage, between the falls and the bridge,
to come up there with a strong, fair wind and a seven-to-eight knot current,
nine times out of ten, your anchor would fail to bring your vessel up,
and she would be forced into the bridge or draw piers damaging one or both.

I have previously stated that for the passage outward,
a fair wind and a high water stockade is necessary *in every case.*
Every cargo of lumber, wood, bark, piling, railroad ties, granite etc
shipped in these vessels would be subjected to a detention of at least 24 hours.
Why? Because a draw in such a bridge could only be passed at high water slack—
and the tide is running OUT at the falls
before it is done running UP at the bridge—
finite things like vessels can only be in *one place* at the *same time.*

So there is but one thing to do, get through the bridge one day,
wait till the next day to go over the falls; no safe anchorage to trust your vessel to,
the wind liable to shift to the Eastward, meanwhile, a storm arise,
your vessel lying between man's invention to destroy you on one side
and God's on the other, and if you escape destruction, you are lucky,
the wind liable to hold for days, in a point where it is impossible
to make the passage of the falls, all the time in danger,
when had it not been for the obstruction
of the bridge, you could have passed the falls the same day
you passed the bridge, as it requires the same wind to stem the current,
and get down to the bridge, that it does to pass the falls.

You understand that frequently there will be a wind
that a vessel could get over the falls with, but the wind don't happen to blow
at the particular time that the tide serves right.
This is particularly so in dog days,
when the wind perhaps will be S.W. in the afternoon,
but high water slack in the falls occurred in the forenoon;
all these things make worse the obstructions that nature has placed in our way,

and argue, with great force against allowing man
to step in and increase our difficulties.
These statements are facts, and with a bridge
the dangers and difficulties would *not* be of rare occurence.

The half has not been said that might be said
against the proposition to bridge tide water above Sullivan Falls.
This much I will say in conclusion:
You can hunt the legislation of this State all through, and in no place,
except in this *one* spot, can you find where a similar outrage
has been committed on whole communities,
under anything like similar circumstances.

—JUSTICE

How I Came Looking for a Poem in the Doorway of a Community Center Where the Voting Lasted All Night in Gambier, Ohio, November 2004

The first snow came fast, a gluey sheet across Ohio, soft earth below,
a sudden snow, northwest along the barns' eaves, rocks bright in the dark stream.
Slashing sleet in Gambier, breath rose from the line standing 10, 12, 16 hours in the
   cold.
There's a sadness when fall breaks into winter with a stab:
sleet drapes the cornstalks, hollow, bent and breaking,
the dusky sheaves downed in rows laid out by horned thumbs and hardened fingertips.

She said it was hard to hold the flimsy punch cards between her still-soft fingertips,
and keep the ballots' chads from falling (like the rain) into muddy pockets below,
spoiling the intention, the purpose she held firm in breaking
dawn (she even brought a stool, no one fooling with her right) and gauzy lightstream.
Shadows cast across broken husks, coats flapping in the stabbing
wind, students wanted to break rank bad and crack glass, but stopped cold.

Rock in hand, the world feels hard, dry and old,
while opening a fist brings stinging blood flow back to fingertips
darkening the palms to plum as pain begins to stab
out a life. Workers scramble on a break, don't see their names on the list below
and jump into pickups to cast ballots at another location, roaring off in a fast stream.
They glare at the line, slowed down to a crawl, have to get back to work, and know they
   are breaking

their word, leaving without voting. NPR will not be carrying the breaking
news: there is nothing new from the touch screen just a return to the same cold
name. Franklin County awarded an extra 4258 votes by counting a healthy stream
four times larger than the tally of voters, maybe wormed up from the dead, these prize
   fingertips
that touched without ever touching the pale green screen below.
Did the worming fingers leave any personal trace or grow larger as they stabbed

into sleek calf skin gloves? Three times I've heard a fight begin, a stab
of anger among friends arguing over whether McCarthy was worse, breaking
the meal into dust as we dropped food below
into sorrow's gut—then stopped. It will take all we have to stay bold
and still allow numb grief to enter without stripping us,
to use darkness and silence to uncover a softer touch, to lift Ohio from its sad dream

bloodying through, a stab at love. How will we find a a rightful stream
of action, familiar as the smell of fingertips ready to take bread and break
pale and dark loaves among strangers in the cold—Ohio.

Flickering

I don't mind 82, 83, 84,
I don't mind being old.
I'm Muriel and I don't mind being old.

One time there was five animals up there on the roof
of the Town Hall and I couldn't figure out
how they got there
til I walked round the other side
and seen the ladder.
So, I figured that out.

Three masted's used to come up in here.
My father was in boats
the men were gone
and my grandfather.

My son comes and stays over sometimes—
he gets hot, so he likes a light cover.
My daughter, she comes down,
stays the night—

I feel better when she comes down.
Some days, I'm good,
then I catch myself
doing too much.

My daughter had a cancer.
They had to do one whole side
then they had to do the other
but she's one who can take it.

When we started out, we didn't have much
and people give us all kindsa clothes.
Now I can do that. There's all kindsa people
needs things, needs things bad.

When the cars go by or the wind's just right,
that little tree between
blows down in the ditch

and I can see right down the bay.
I went down there
to the Historical,
took my lunch in a basket.
Oh, they used me good, didn't need no questions.

Some nights, the cars come along the curve by the Historical
and something inside gets to flickering.
Don't know what it is, but Jeepers, I've had an awful good
time watching that flickering.

I'm Muriel Stanhope
and I can see between.

Smoke

Exhale Dad, salesman Dad driving across the top of New York state. Late at night, window rolled down, sleeves rolled up, smoking. Fat books of carpet samples tossed in the back of the Ford wagon. Time falling at the heels of his tires as he turns towards the hoop of the golden summer moon on the horizon. He's proud of the good time he's made, takes another pack down from behind the visor. Smoke, the signal of his return. He enters the house, pats down his jacket, hangs it loosely on the back of the office chair, and pulls out the end of the pack of Chesterfields. He lays the crumpled pack on top of the desk, silver lighter touching the cellophane. Makes last notes legible for his morning meeting. Comes to the beds of the children, waking to the smell of the long trip, hungry for the smoke of the kiss, collapsing with slurring nigh,nigh. Cigarette resting on green glass shelf below the bathroom mirror, gray eyes looking back at darker shadows under the eyes. He throws cold water on his face, still holding the drive, washes his hands with scalding water, works a lather up over his thumbs. Hands left dripping catch a white towel, lift and expunge the oils of his skin, as he circles the contours of his forehead, cheekbones, fingers dipping under the jawline to meet briefly at his chin. He takes a last draw, careful not to burn his fingers, presses it between his lips, eyes squinting as smoke wafts upwards. Cigarette butt hisses into toilet with a flick of the wrist. He pulls the book off the back of the toilet and sits—reading. He lets the words float upwards and surround him—a new direction growing outside the headlight's gleam. Only night watches, heat streaming in the window. He goes to the shared bed, sees his wife stirring under the blanket, and leans in, nuzzle of day-old beard, gray sheen slightly damp in the dark.

The Colt

We drew against each other, even if I just play-drew. I mimicked from my ghost double holsters, the two forty-fives or I had the bright silver, light-weight model with the fake blond ivory, brown-bone texture carved into the sides. I learned to fan—up and down with the outside of my palm against the hammer—keeping the motion steady, keeping the gunfire rapid, losing no time with an upsweep but hardening the back of my hand and peeling off another round.

He beat me to the draw. He had the gun. I'd be the dead man, even though he loved to fall, wounded, rising up on one knee then finishing me off as I lifted my head, but I'd rise too, saying the bullet nicked my rib, glanced off, and lying on my side in the dust, I'd surprize him. Holding the handle with both hands, I'd squeeze off another round. Flying back from the power of the shot, he'd hit the wall and begin his slow slide down, holding his 'shattered' shoulder—not dead but stricken, he'd grimace and sink to his knees where he'd get a surge of last-minute strength and we'd begin again playing out all the forms of wounding.

Brown leather holster with a flourish carved on the side housed the six-shooter—later the plain black leather holster, gun of steely gray, the real one. He wanted the ivory handle but couldn't get it. He ordered from a catalogue—got the authentic Colt with the form-fit molded grip, very hard black plastic, stripped down he called it. He was 15, I was almost 11. I touched the grip, but never held the weight of the gun in my hands.

From my room across the hall, I could hear him reach for it, reach for his gun. Working on his fast-draw—draw, cock, aim and holster. I mirror him across the hall in my imagination. Holsters strapped on backwards, he draws fancy, wrist over wrist, hands crossed. Blowing smoke from the tip, he spins the barrel, holsters the gun. Ptchoo, ptchoo, k-bam, k-bam, I hear him dive and slide mopping the floor with his flannel shirt. He practices late, past my falling into sleep.

I wanted to be fast, but he had the gun. I learned to run, hit the sidewalk and ran, over the laid brick rising and falling like a dusty red river, the pattern of roots spreading like a giant hand under the sidewalk.

Prelude to My Father's Never Dying Again

I have often felt as if I were inside my father's skin--that we communicate our similarities physically—by gesture, by a kind of quiet, by the pattern of the exasperated breath in the wake of frustration following the chorus of escalating curses—"Hell's Bells; Jesus Pesus" and held in reserve for a particularly absurd self-mockery, "Jesus, Mary and Joseph." This is never the end of the line, but the lighting of the slow fuse, the charge of breath that brings the fire up. Even-temperedness is something my father and I share--though his is a matter of faith, even belief, and mine, a fine-honed passion.

Now, there is the still-fresh fact that he is dead, fresh as if the ground cannot close over him. Free associating does not come easily, withers next to the need for his physical mark, the yearning to hear evidence of his presence. And there is my insistent embodiment as I say no. Always no, he will never be dead for me followed by waves surging across the long lake of sorrow that lives in my chest. Tilted at times like a walking stick or a feather-light canoe, blond in the water, and last of all, the stream of love exclaiming through the pen that must flow to keep him alive.

There is no way around it—how terribly I miss him once I begin to ask: where is he now and who is he to me? I get out the pen and begin circling the boulder—his forehead in the sun, darkening brown and furrowing as he surveys his garden and releases a thin airy whistle of concentration that pours from his lips as he digs deep in April's cold mud readying the ground for annuals. As vivid as he is to me, I know I will never penetrate the rock, the lake and the stick; nor how it is we wear the same golden skin in the sun, how we carry the relief and worry of the shade, and a cool grace housed in quiet.

When I am 15, I lie in the recovery room in a hospital bed, angry, alive, and full of the seasoned hope that brightens the blood when the body alone is in charge and the mind can do nothing but hum—remembering, listening, absorbing, but unable to speak. I am not alone. There are thirty others on the children's ward—all under 14—and there is my father who comes every day to be with me. Sometimes he reads the paper and sometimes he just sits quietly, while I listen to his breath.

I resisted the anaesthesia mightily—sodium penathol in both arms and finally, the sweet gas over my face as I stopped counting backwards from 100 at 85. Sure they were trying to kill me, when they said the surgery would fix me, I thought I was being altered like a cat or dog. They were fixing me to put an end to the unpredictable rebelliousness that now came from my every pore, determined only to break every rule and leave behind any standing relationship to family, friends and school.

I wake in a thickness of sounds, bodies not words. We are coming out from under and send up messages, banners that snap in the room above us, messages of pride, sinewy and strangely peopled as we shout out names we will not remember. I sit up, fall back among the mouths, open sounding, and listen to the dull hammering of bodies finding the bars on the bedsides. I turn to face a man's back, stitched and cut and stitched and cut. I flop the other way, press my head against cold bars, throw up on the floor. My hands move to my stomach and stroke two tubes. I tug drowsily, angrily, I am patted back into the sheets, as my hands fly away from me. "When you can tell us what time it is, we'll take you to your ward." I sleep. When I wake, I search for the clock's hands—the large white face somewhere on the wall. 12:45, 6:30, 9:11, 10:19, I yell.

I wake in the hospital room where there are four of us: so much further away, the inside of my lids, a huge map of the red world, the closest I can come to the light, to events, to motion. Deep in my blood thrum, I race as part of a vast populace—I feel so small, yet believe in my blood, its music that hurtles and calls. If only you could see. No one would believe I could be so small and still hear the motion of the world. I must work on gaining a largeness around my slippery pulse, a body who can re-enter this life. I need all my strength— even my skin, miles off as it is, must hold. I am glad to be here. If only I could tell you. I must work to get there--before I can see you, touch you, speak to you. You will not see me, I know, until I am well. But I am here, just under and all over my skin.

My father is the first to come. My eyes open now and I know that scares him—I still don't have the strength to talk. He sits in the heat, the blinds slitting the light, his suit soaked under the arms, behind his knees. He has left work early, peels himself off the chair, then sits down again. I want to tell him how much I love him sitting there breathing, smelling like cigarettes, clearing his throat with his hat in his hand and his fine graying hair creased from the hat band. He fans the heavy air then settles again. The air he is touching touches me. He is my father. And we are mingling our silence.

Whenever he arrives, I hear him—first in the hall, clearing his throat. It starts in a low repeating, a sound like a kid imitating machine-gun fire, but softly, and ends in a swallowed neighing. His quietness follows him everywhere. He is peering in at me, through the heat, Boston summer, his neck coming forward slowly, the creases smoothing on his large boned brow, tan and beaded with sweat, his tortoise shell glasses hard against his face, his eyes, a very dark blue, lit somehow from the inside. Sometimes his hands fly to his eyes and he quickly brushes back his tears like hair, resettles his glasses with the spread of one hand, squares them against his brow as if his face needed to see more and he was starting again in earnest, a newcomer to the world.

Children's Ward, Mass General

Rope of light, hand over hand, returns.
Spiraling down the tunnel of sodium pentothal, rising into hard daylight
sitting straight up, music of moans, the glass shield, the johnny and the draft
of hospital air across my body, carved, and carving across the sweet desert of spring,
   blood
surging health in the flowers. Soft golden triangle of pubic hair shaved to avoid
   infection grows
back stronger, darker—where is my glow I sometimes had?

I hear the child crying   through the night   through the day
something strong and urgent beyond my waving self—
why hasn't anyone come? I see her night cries shaping the shadows overhead
as I lie on my back and blue flags spiral through the wall.
She sends them high on the wind of her ragged breath.
She has a power like the wind but no direction.
Why is she here and why is she entering my room like this?
I can't rise to see her directly, but I dream her and I ask who she is and where she came
   from.
I can't hold the answer from the dream, but I hold her
all day in my intravenous arms, quiet by my side.

When I can walk, I go next door to visit and see a baby in two leg casts, bulbs
that don't move but stick straight out. I want to take away the flag of dread
I feel planted in her room. There wasn't much I could say to the nurse
who let me in, except thanks. I stood silently and tried growing hope inside
and making it big enough for both of us. I thought she needed a lot.
I cut through and asked for help.
I didn't ask, I thundered.
The nurses said I was in a real mood.

When her cries came swimming overhead again, her turtle shadow,
I knew the rain would come, I could smell it, and her wounds too were sealing up.
She already knew how to float and I could see that her bandages
would come off in the grinding salt waves of her own life.
This was something I could believe in.

Messages from Sea: 1943

1. No Litany of Light

He smoked in his quarters, in the hold, at the small desk where he typed up the log each
   week. He made an ashtray out of a shell casing and had to punish Brock for lighting
   up on deck—a match behind a cupped hand in broad daylight.

No sign of light. No flame to cigarette,
no steady hand kept level
watching tobacco flakes curl and catch.
No cupped hand. No deep inhale. No raised
ribcage. No smile or o-shaped lips.
No stream of smoke, flood of worries
exhaled into the air. No
symbol passed, no language of light.
No visible means of detection.
No solo watch and thinking moon.
No shared past. No spark
of recognition, talking it over.

Darkness. The waves slap,
uncontained by darkness.
Feel the steady engine of men:
what dreams pattern the roads
imagined in the hunger for land.

2. Censor

All action becomes a prayer of hands
converging at the prow—fingertips like candles,
guns at the ready, portholes blacked out.
Behind the black paint
my father reads
letters home from the Navy men
delivered unsealed to his door.
He is the official censor, cuts out
location, place names, destinations,
flow of cargo passing quickly under his hands.
He takes a razor, cuts
a slot in the page where the words fall
then burns small papers in the brass ashtray
made from a cartridge shell.
He is the interrupter of speech, texture
and breath across the mind. He gets good
at skimming, quickly riding each man's rhythm
of speech, yearning, incident, streams
of thought, so he can read less carefully as time goes on.
He doesn't like knowing the shapes of thought
behind their young masks.
He seals the mail,
sends it out across the water.

3. Letter X

We passed within a few miles of my brother Geoff the other morning. I could see the dark bulk of land and the lights blinking as the shapes of the ships passed between me and shore. But, of course, I could do nothing... a queer feeling of frustration. I would love to speak freely with someone, not that I have anything to get off my chest, but to talk with the mask down would be a great satisfaction. 'Mask' is a poor word, 'guard' is a little better. What I mean, I think, is that I don't really know my companions and I am afraid of boring or annoying them with talk of me or my family or you or my work. All the Captain wants of me, basically, is to know that the guns, gunners and ammunition are ready. Beyond that, the Navy and my private life are only as interesting as I can make them in anecdote.

4. What Has Been Cut

They hold Robbie between them
tracing the lines of hair
greased dark from running sweat
as Robbie turns himself out
spilling to Charles' cupped jaw, the play
of the moon drawing down
their ropey silhouette on deck:
Jim's arms hooked through
Robbie's elbows. Charles in a crouch,
his brow absorbed in the shadow of Robbie's flexing
thighs. Splayed fingers open and close and begin on Jim
kneading a small circle outward through the dark looping crisscross of hair.

Nothing to Hide

in memory of Assotto Saint

I was born caged with love,
and I have an infinite
amount to show,
so I wear a coat
that turns out, the way tulips like to do.

Tulip, I insist on saying your name,
Tulip, I insist on being hauled from the ground
in a tight gray glove, a curling fist
sent straight to the sun's rays.
I keep it up—and who's counting—for a month,
bobbing in the air, more modest and choosey at night,
and splayed open at noon to all of Rome,
then petal by petal, triumphant,
drop, bloody drop-dead gorgeous.

Ten Minutes
for Hettie Jones & in memory of Fielding Dawson

1.

We went into the women's high security correctional facility
to teach a poetry workshop—
we were on the same clock
but not on the same time
as the women keep inside.
"Fire hazard" can confiscate your poetry,
notes for an appeal and all your books.

Inside, time is an emptiness
more than a movement
as hours flow down the bones,
sweat moves on its own,
covers your own unmistakable
beautiful curving shape in its own unmistakable odor,
but time is handed down by someone else.
The bones slow down to keep up with the hours.

There was no call out list,
no call out for the women
to leave their cells,
nothing left inside, no mark
on paper providing the right information
to allow us space in a room
at a time designated for the purpose of giving a poetry workshop—
a place of air and bright paper, scratched deep into a different sky.

Questions from outside are not ok—
we were caught off-guard,
there was no place, since none was identified.
No room for the workshop.
We were cleared and let in,
neither one of us cleared to be this far
talking to the guard outside the college center
without a call out.
He rattled the drawers of his desk looking—
told us, "There's no call out."
We stood and waited having breached security

standing in the basement corridor
of lemon-yellow cinder blocks with picture windows
looking into the vacant nursery and empty rooms.
How could that happen? everyone wondered aloud inside.

The Deputy Superintendent
was coming down to escort us out
from the hallway of the college center
where we had been known, regularly seen, assumed to be all right
on other days, when the women came crowding down the hill
working a whirlpool motion, so the talk can swirl and rise
and land where it needs to go. Some stay quiet on the side waiting for a word,
while others do a zig-zag weave and make up for lost time in loud circling,
covering the fast and low, inside the stream of voices.
Tonight, there were no women outside the mailroom
jostling on the bench waiting for packages, when we went in,
no voices in the nursery.
It was quiet.

All the women were in their cells.
We waited.
I wasn't sure what we didn't have or why we didn't have it.
It felt like too long a story and no time to tell it—
know what I mean?

   2.

There was no call out, no call out
for the women to leave
their cells
and we had no way to leave word,
speak
to the women or leave a sign.
We were stranded or separated from our purpose
like most people inside, except
if you're from outside,
you are never
stranded in prison.
You are escorted unless you have a non-escort pass
with a picture id and we had id's with pictures
clipped and hanging from our necks.
The Deputy Superintendent

marched us down the corridor
and right back out.

A forbidden something-or-other, a word or two, had escaped.
A word or two can create a crisis, a threat to security,
and the effects, much like a hurricane,
were still being measured. The action required to secure
the prison had to be swift. Discipline had to be restored
and punishment had to demonstrate unquestionable authority
within the prison and within the correctional system
all the way to the top. We heeded the call for silence.

There were words, being held ready in the cells
for the space or the blank page,
to release a sharp breath and fill the lungs with bright blood.
All we could do was keep quiet and breathe
if we ever hoped to get back in again.

3.

The lock-down had an exact date and time and was set in accordance with the
    procedures that follow the escape of forbidden news. Once the lock-down is set into
    motion, it moves in its own time and space and just has to play out.
It comes from above.
It takes as long as it takes, so they didn't bother, as the noose tightened,
to check that there might have been an unexpected two
who slipped in on the last sunbeam reflecting off the day's door.
Guided by that refracting ray dancing down the hall, and not getting
that we started the day thinking we had something to give,
and we were happy about it, we were smiling inside and out
which is always a mistake inside.

Censoring doesn't really have an end date
in terms of a strict following of the rules and regs
whereby any threat considered serious
has a date begun and a date done, so it was really only a matter of time
before the unsaid, the unexpected and the imagined
would meet in a direct head-on,
When the prison went into lock, we were made of air.
Our names were not written at the top of the lovely sounding
rounded names on the non-existent call-out list for a poetry workshop.

Across the weary tiles and looking up at the yellow walls,
we heard breathing.
Breath being taken in and breath let go
coming from the cells of the women on that spring night.
The cells held
an expectation of speech
and the newest procedures for lock
pinned words to the roof
of the mouth
and took effect in the time it takes to start a poem
in your mind and maybe mull a first line, jot it down.
Minutes before we arrived, words rose inside
and began to press slowly from the flesh and emit
a light sweat growing darker.

We heard silence sweat—all the women in their cells locked down.

    4.

We followed behind the broad back of the Dep, her steady steps,
and the guards turned their mouths
back in and back down to a very high steady quiet alert.
We signed in at 6 pm and out at 6:10.
We could not read the names, and our shadows could not be seen
as we leaned away from the too-bright light falling across the sign-in desk.
We walked out into the parking lot and out into the night,
the sound of our steps annihilated by the echo at our backs.

Call   call call   there's no call
call   call
out.

Outlines

I don't want to go on proving how broken
    we are   shredding the stars
               in the vast night sky

The woods are black and white today
    snow living on the branches   holding in the light dry cold

Purple burly trunk
        faint orange seams—
           the flush between scales
               light of pine passing through

Looking into the forest
        as if the sun stood
        at the core of every grove.

The Bear

for Marie Ponsot on the occasion of her 80th birthday
and for Anna Dembska on her 70th birthday

Bear breaks cover in March, brushing through snow.
Cold dust rises as he sweeps by low bushes, buried garden,
crystals freeze edging the black nose.

He heads for the sprawling human house,
hungry and yearning to bury it all again,
in the gut, the hold.

Bird feeder on a pole.
Bear boxes with bird feeder
glass cracks, seeds flood the white surface
rod pulled to one side
seeds like water.
Bear shovels down the catch, seeds like trout
bouncing down the throat.

Tracking the bear backwards
to see where it all began
I have soon lost the bear who found the last apple on the hill.

Bear's hunger walks the road fast, down the hill, faster, unencumbered.

*

Bear wakes in the eye of green apple dream—
the shine, shape, air and smell
of summer
leaves rushing ahead.

Light refracted on the snow
as he rises to search the dream of time and what's left—
frozen, dried on the stalk, juice, any juice—
the ground hard, white impenetrable—
the ground, the ground, his bowl, the ground.

Bear rips, shears apple wood—
insects frozen fast inside,

breaks the edge of ice to haul up sleeping sacks
of fish buried in the muck.

                *

Blue jays make greedy all winter—
rushing noise and wings—
tell the bear to go where the humans live.
The humans live in pits of food
and heave it around themselves in larger
and larger circles— food—road—food—road—food-road.

The humans know
little of the dark, how
to find the way through it.

Silence of snow
packed against bear's nested fur, his ears—
then the humans move it all around
so food-road can rule again.

Towards April
melting melting
mud delicious in the claws

                *

The bear woke, rose away from leaves
and needles, husks,
rose out of the curling orbit
away from the imprint of thick fur
packed tight against the inside
of the earth.

Bear swung down the crest of hill
and clipped the last apple—bruisie-brown—
from the deepening night of the tree.
He pawed upwards in the air, backed off—
grabbed, shook—
the apple fell through the snow sinking far below.

Bear bellows, brown orb dislodged
then fast bear

bucket claw
hooked apple.

Pawing upwards, the bear touches all the stars
that have fallen sunken in the ground,
lighting crystals in the snow.
Apple juice runs
in the roof of his mouth, stars.

Translations from *The Poems of Vikram Babu* by Jesús Aguado (2008)
by Electa Arenal / Beatrix Gates

Como hormigas en fila:
                  un yo que se disgrega
necesita encontrar un agujero,
una envoltura,
              un nombre,
eso que tan ufanos denominamos mundo.

Vikram Babu pregunta:
                  ¿tú también?

Like the long line of ants in single file:
                    an I detached
must find a hole,
shelter,
        a name,
what we so proudly call the world.

Vikram Babu asks:
                    you too?

Como el que mata a un niño y lo desuella
y machaca sus huesos
                    y quema sus tendones
y da a comer sus vísceras a un perro

y, orgulloso, convoca
a pades, familiares y vecinos,
ls explica con lujo de detalles
su cruel comportamiento
y luego les invita a que entre todos
armen de nuevo el puzzle de ese niño.

Vikram Babu pregunta:
                    ¿eres así?

Like the one who kills then skins a child,
grinds its bones,
                burns its tendons,
feeds the guts to the dog—

full of pride he calls a meeting
of parents, relatives and neighbors,
explains in unswerving detail
the minutiae of his cruel acts
and then requests that the community
puzzle the child back together again.

Vikram Babu asks:
                are you like that?

Como esas caravanas que van por el desierto
y sólo se detienen a ofrecer
sus mercancias
                en los espejismos.

Y qué raro:
                obtienen
gran rentabilidad.

Vikram Babu pregunta:
                ¿ qué llevan sus camellos?

Like those caravans that travel across the desert
and stop only to offer
their merchandise
                        at the mirages.

How strange:
                  they turn
a great profit.

Vikram Babu asks:
                        what do their camels carry?

Como el rey que construye en palacio de vidrio,
los muros, las estancias transparentes,
no hay secretos, pues todo
está bien a la vista para todos,
y al principio era un juego pero luego
el rey se siente incómodo
y en vez de hacerlo opaco con cortinas
o muros interiores,
                            cualquier cosa,
ordena vaciar los ojos de sus súbditos.

Vikram Babu pregunta:
                            ¿eres así?

Like the king who builds a glass palace,
the walls, the rooms transparent.
There are no secrets—everything
can be seen by everyone.
It began as a game
but the king becomes uncomfortable
and instead of closing the palace off with curtains,
interior walls,
         or anything at all,
he orders his subjects' eyes gouged out.

Vikram Babu asks:
        are you like that?

Como el que va una boda
                    tan sucio que le expulsan,
y prueba en otra puerta
                    y le azuzan los perros,
y desgarra la lona de la tienda
y entre varios le atrapan y ke arrojan
volando a las letrinas,
y prueba a hacer un túnel
y las ratas le muerden las orejas.

Todo en vez de asearse,
                    de ponerse otras ropas,
quizás algo de sándalo
                    y aceite para el pelo,
O una guirnalda.
            Cosas sencillas.
                        Sobre todo
si tenemos en cuenta
                    que era su propia boda.
Vikram Babu pregunta:
                ¿quién se casa?

Like the one who goes to a wedding
                    so filthy that he is thrown out
and tries to get in through another door
                    and the dogs bark at him,
and he tears the tent canvas
and it takes several people to get hold of him and toss him
flying into the bathroom
where he tries to dig a tunnel
and the rats bite his ears.

Anything not to clean up
                    put on other clothes
a scent of sandalwood perhaps
                    oil on his hair
a flower.
            Simple things
                              Especially
considering
                    it was his own wedding.
Vikram Babu asks:
                    who wants to get married?

Como el dulce leproso que cantaba
poemas encendidos a sus muchos muñones
e invitaba a besarlos
con tan firme alegría que nadie se negaba.

Vikram Babu pregunta:
                    ¿quién te crees
que entretiene en el cielo
                    ahora con sus bailes
a tanto dios inválido?

Like the gentle leper who sang
incandescent poems to his many stumps
inviting tender kisses for them
with such convincing joy that no one could refuse.

Vikram Babu asks:
                           who do you think
provides glorious entertainment
                           with his dances now
for so many disabled gods in heaven?

Como aquel que construye una escalera
con humo de un incendio.
Peldaños, pasamanos:
                    todo es humo.

Va al mercado a venderla.
                    Pero nadie
se atreve a dar ni un paso:
tienen miedo a caerse si al hacerlo
de pronto se disipa.
A alguien que fuera de humo le vendría
perfecta esta escalera:
                    a alguien ya muerto,
                                        a un loco,
a un ermitaño,
                a un dios,
a una de esas montañas aburridas
que sueñan con bajar al animso valle,
a cualquiera que lleve cien años ayunando.

(Del humo de un incendio fabricó la escalera
que ascienden y descienden
                    sus ojos cuando miran,
sus manos cuando tocan,
                su boca cuando come,
su espalda cuando duerme
y sus palabras siempre,
                    cuando habla o cuando calla).

Y ya todos se han ido del mercado.
Y brilla la escalera en medio del vacío,
tremolando en la noche.
Y llega entonces Nadie y se la compra,
y Nadie se la compra.

Vikram Babu pregunta:
                    ¿cuánto pides?

Like the one who makes a ladder
from the smoke of a fire.
Rungs, rails:
                   all is smoke.

He goes to the market to sell it.
                        But no one
dares take a single step:
they are afraid of falling through
if suddenly it vanishes.
For someone made of smoke
it would be perfect, this ladder:
                    for one long dead
                              for one gone mad,
a hermit,
            a god,
or one of those bored mountains
that dreams of descending to the animated valley,
or for anyone who has been fasting for a hundred years.

(From the smoke of a fire he fabricated the ladder
his eyes travel up and down
                    when they look,
his hands when they touch,
                    his mouth when he eats
his spine when he sleeps
and his words always
                    when he speaks or is still.)

Now everyone has left the market place.
The ladder shines in the emptiness,
Trembling in the night.
Then Nobody comes and buys it from him,
and Nobody buys it from him.

Vikram Babu asks:
                    how much are you asking?

Dos (2014)

Epiphany
for Electa on January 6th

Blue bowl and the coming light
high maples glow red-tipped at dawn
full gesture of blood returning to limbs,
the threat of a surprising golden wind.
I am the coming bright
side of the triangle, hold myself
folded against my ribs, hands
uneasily preparing for all the feelings
to resurface on my skin.
Tight gray bark awash,
dark stain of sudden thaw—
all I need exposed in winter light:
the new old roots that deepen
as love calls up—*urgente*—
and the entire body answers
until all movement is
built on fierce joy and alarming patience,
lips daily grazing
the tenderness that surrounds me—this that has become
what I cannot do without:
it is asked of me
again even as winter is upon us
and it cannot be stopped, this asking
of the body to trust,
to carry the change to every outer reach
until present touch
touches present.

Dos

I. The Painting

When I saw the painting on the wall:
all black, volcanic tags curling inside the cone,
I knew her.   Touched by her sleeping core

I opened the wall and walked in.

I sought the molding of earth,
while the volcano grew larger sound within.

The lava
hard, soft
killing chain
that molds in highest heat
then cools and fits an iron collar.

Facelessness awaited, obliteration
indistinct, perpetual—the volcano
could take the mountainside
and turn it into a crater of dust,
shake a forest to sticks.

Leaping sun, the fire I craved to understand
drew me, pulled within, lava crust fed by lava
growing forms
as massive plates shifted under a ropey sea, and smoke rose in a wisp.

Lava covered the traces
as I danced on the open pores of earth—
my life, a shadow dance, throwing light behind.

The longing does not end.
The interior will not be read.

Fire burns everything but the bones
writing past any ending as they
enter earth and die there.

I arrived into the darkness,
I arrived into the heat.
I was there before the light,
before I could see the outline of her face,
her moon brow, high ribs and hips rising

If I moved slowly, she stayed
and if she moved quickly, I made no sudden gesture.
I matched breath for breath
calling the bird back: desire and flight.

I thought I wanted to live in her darkness
I thought I wanted to live in her violet throat
altering breath   blue dusk red,
husky toned explosion frayed green gold and scarlet dawn.

Is beauty a gift or a one-eyed center,
the eye, unseeing of others, and unknown to itself, the eye
awed and stunted from force of attention?
And who is blinded most by the gift—arrow or target, seeker or sought?

I was there when the sun left again
for the other side   I looked into the earth
for fire to light the way   I turned from the sky, stars all.
Facelessness awaited, beauty burned.   Volcano.

What bird of fire leaves the crust of the earth
smoking in skirts of lava, grows plummage of paradise
to carry all colors of the sun into the crater-sunken world?

I felt nothing leave me   not skin or time
    I did not see
                my crumbling shadow
as I moved back to the City, a place without sky whose brightness fills the void,
    to live with her.

Fire burned everything except the bones
and I lived in her darkness: touch brilliant,
shining from coal eyed quiet.

How to guard life within,
a shell minding the hollow, flushed by the tides
and curving towards return.
I could not enter my own home
without losing myself to hers.

To live in the dissembled
power of the tender
floating ash.   Volcano.

We met in a doorway
   seen and seeing, gentle one cheek kiss.

   Life spread out, dry wandering root,
   not having yet found the way.
   A passage closing: I saw her and crossed
   demanding to see my face in raw, untended light
   demanding she meet her own running shadow
   in burning air
   where all shadows run together.

The fire door closed, fire roared to high heat.

Isn't that how it is: the opening of one life
   to another—opposites each becoming
   larger than the other—the other larger
   before love is an idea?

  Some time later, I stopped.   Taking in.   To live.
    The longing does not end.

To stand quiet, full shadow cast behind,
   unafraid of another's light or dark
   and feel the full-throated sun, lemon yellow red,
   ride the sky all day and fall through the night
   into further circles of cool immensity.

   Fearsome secret, our shy turning
   to the sky as years return us

and pass
outside earth span.

Is it the bird of death I ride
taking my body, ribbed kite,
as I fly   inside the far moment?

II. The Knife

The cut.
She used it as a verb,
"when we cut...."

As a girl, she survived the knife
when her abuelita challenged her, Take it!
handing her the knife,
the morning she announced she wanted to end her life,
Take it!
as the girl turned away in shame,
shame for her life and shame for admitting the pain of it
to her grandmother, her father's own
supreme protector, mother.

Live your own life, not someone else's—scar knot we shared.
I turned to arrive into a different language, hers.
I wanted to taste the sound, alive in my mouth,
and pull the cut closed with a song.

Years before, I let a boy slice my neck to see what it was like.
A young girl—my answer, Yes.
Luck the cut that left a need for song,
and from then on, I heard the white throated sparrow's
four notes as my own Yes, no no no... .

The girl in Mexico watched the machete come down
on the necks of the chickens slaughtered in the kitchen,
taken squawking from the henhouse
next to the house on the roof where she and her mother and sister stayed,
feathers drifting on steamy air
and landing on stones in the street below,
roosters crowing from the chimney and gutters
of her grandmother's boarding house.

The girl tasted the sharp burst of saliva in the mouth of disdain,
and acrid silence in the hall
where she ran the length of stairs
passing her father's second floor rooms
shared with another woman. She,
later listed as his wife in the books, a mention
of two children, and none of her own mother
whose hand she held, sometimes,
when the three—mother and two daughters—
walked three abreast upstairs.

Second language, she heard Spanish first, but learned to speak English,
and before her native tongue cleared, strange numbers
appeared on the blackboard: continuing relationship, a mystery to the girl
between languages, erased at the end of each school day
by close mother English and kitchen Spanish—
grandmother supervising the count.

The girl danced, spoke in a rush of skipping words
and counted steps, cobbled stones
and letters of her mother's name, Rose,
and letters in her father's name, Luis,
the same count and same broken syllables in Spanish.

It seemed to her that only birds in flight could sing
the same way in all syllables
as they trilled shapes dancing on air.

   III. The Head

The sculpture sits silent, remembering.
Visible from all directions, the head of Benito Juarez
rises from across the plane.
The globe looks out and looks back,
while being seen alone, stranded on the flats of a sprawling suburban frieze.
The sky curves away.

Mexico is within sight:
horizon unblocked on an unremarkable day,
save for the live memory
that would come darkening

as the people moved to open the lines,
and take the tracks, fully loaded, to the city.
Some remembered Juarez for what he tried to do:
Mexico, first and last.

From the five directions, people confront the monument
to Juarez every day, unmarked, fading into dusky concrete.

Behind the brow, a glorious, hidden observatory in the brain of Juarez,
sunken, old, unmoving eyes that saw and see still:
all of Mexico. Juarez: the first to seize
property tear Church from state.
   He did not win.
   He did not lose.
   He moved towards the doors
   and he opened them with his entire being
   like the doors of the sun.

He stood on the horizon in exile and on return
and he wrote and spoke from the sun-washed mountains

Unheralded stranger from an indigenous tribe,
when he landed, blue/brown rock on the yellow earth,
his agate eyes breathed through the shaking desert,
Sierra Madre de Oaxaca, Sierra de Ixtlan, Sierra Monteflor,
Sierra Madre del Sud.
He saw human lives, still
without enough food, water or work.
To be able to feed every citizen,
to feed the earth

Benito Juarez corresponded with Lincoln.
The people knew they had a leader and demanded he lead.
From under the globe, they began to walk in the hot dust
of his footsteps and celebrate his tenacity. Even as exile
drew blood from his cause, he was not forgotten:
he counted the human number of their lives.

Iron will and golden tongue of Juarez, transmuted,
Mexico took the horizon like the sun—red warning to white-gold blare of noon
and orange swath cinching down the dark—
hunger aleved, people embraced the right to grow
a full life long, into a blue edged evening.

Mexico knew the meaning
of the cool knife of Benito Juarez's mind:
he wrote a constitution.
A federation, life-long sun on the mountains,
shining at the edge of day.

The Benito Juarez head
placed on the earth like a ball:
motion lives inside the monument as expectation.
Blood pumps to the veins below
and into the double caverns of the heart.

Geometry defined the plane and defied the plane
and from under the globe, the sky curved away
and everything else stayed red, brown   beating under the ground.

It was her father Luis, the sculptor who created the Juarez head,
and he who fled, untouchable
curving path, dark star spinning away to another world.
She began to dance.

We went together to see the dome rising from the plane—
she had the same rounded sun brow, her father's,
and the landed, other worldly sculpture—exact
replica down to the parted lips
and viewing station behind plated eyes.

Looking up around the head's dome,
a reminder of a picture she kept in the hallway:
Luis' wide forehead in the sun,
dark frame glasses squaring oval eyes,
cigarette smoke, the mate to a mild manner,
while bold woodcuts fell from the bone,
fingers carving fire racing across the field,
   women running, rifle butts slung inside rebozos,
   muzzles angled forward   wheat and corn forward
   smoke blowing back.   He had to look back to see.

Across the sky at sunset, the head of Juarez
goldens like her skin and her father's,
uncounted daughter, named for his mother

as if that name was enough for a blood line to cross the desert and survive
all the way to north america.

When we see the sculpted head,
the father shines.
And from her same patch of earth, close or far in time,
his absence shines.

He cut the fingers, one by one,
from the hand
that grasped
for his.

Mother held the girls
by the hand,
and when they asked where their father was,
and then who he was,
she answered: his art.

He slid past down the face of the cliff
marrying twice more
then coiling peacefully at the bottom like rope
into his own circle.

He turned easily from stone carving to wood mallet
to plaster cast to paint and then back to black
and white. He said carving wood blocks always gave him
painting back, brought yearning to his fingertips.
Rope twisted to splatter paint, three wives
helped him stay alive.

Five arches below the Juarez head,
a span secured so the globe could float
above the ground   the shape of human thought
stark on the horizon, a warning and triumph.
A human scale for Mexico.

The Juarez head waits.

Five doors to enter in
  to leave through
  Earth doors.

The head becomes the earth's brow

Earth thinking in her own good time,
ready for vision to be occupied again
for the male idea to become the woman.

Juarez waits quietly for his mother, his father, the earth.

The sculptor opens the earth.

The sculptor opens the earth with every stroke of peeling air
cut from stone, held in a mold, cast back into hardened cement—
he saw the city as part of the vision
and wanted Juarez within view.
The sculptor nowhere to be found.

He landed the meteoric head,
sun and wind outside the cavernous eyes,
a notched balcony across the the monumental brow.
The sculptor knows there can be no one person inside.

The daughter too knows there can be no one person inside
a political movement or a life.

Today the fire door
takes nothing in.

No more father shadow dance
threat, envy, abandonment.

Now metal door heart
is secure.

She could only trace her father's adhering absence.
Blood and bone stuck to boots,
revolutionary wounds across time,
his leaving a replica, a larger than life skull, behind.

Cut the aorta at the neck

or flatten the vein with a boot. Stand on the neck,
as blood winds to the heart
a half breed grown under the desert
and vining to the city's ancient aquifer.
Mexico will provide a place for her
and clear water, a daughter, not half of anything but Mexican.

I turn the lights off,
because I trust only my basic instincts now.
I reach for the handle in the dark.

I find the fire door. It is open.
Now I know the way out.

    IV. Inside the Wind

The taste of her dries, evaporates sweet
inside the wind and stays like salt.
Sun   how you carry waves on the air
      I listened for your cold dawn anchor
      part of her staying as part of her sailed.

Wind   the dusky voiced companion,
   as clouds
      covered and uncovered her eyes:
I hold her by letting her run through my hands.

I learn to sing
death lives here:
the deeper the love
the deeper the pain, her words.

Fire-torn husk   I fell to red earth.
  Fire burns everything except the bones.

Twisted sticks tap on shelves of rock
   picked up by the wind
     ochre slabs cut with blue scrawling words
until veins can be seen again.

Carved grief   voice of blackened sands.
Bare rock before and after,
she sought a teller
for her storied self
hoping someone else could tell
what the wind said before tearing it from her mouth.

She grew herself on the air
    and burnished talons for landing.

Gryphon bisexual: she could not fail the test
    of pride
and power would be hers
    in flight.

Brow turned upward
taking in the sun:
her cinnamon skin glows at dusk,
her grandmother's
Tabascena knives and blood
under hoof prints at the edge of the desert.

Skeletal ash for miles,
the blood volcano's glistening sash.
Air, the only name for life.

    V. Answer

I didn't really want to talk about it or tell,
taking my life up again, my good feet
walking backwards
    across hot deaf stones, then running until I reached a cave,
        the artist's room.   The whole of it, weighing too much,
until that moment when all her unanswering (silence) lay deep
in my slowly turned back, weeping done.

There. I burned all the papers, I spoke to the wall alone. I said it.
I threw it away to survive. Don't make me do it again.

My friend said: some have given up.
    You gave what you had   you loved.

She is the I I loved.

She the stranger I could almost become
and when I floated alone, a stranger,

I found others
who in kindness asked me,
across the ground of powdery ash and shapes of dying selves
who are you?

I learned to love by being stranded
where the current and the tide, and loneliness itself,
neither hers   nor mother brine   was my salt answering sea.

Wide-lit morning
red shout of evening
she who expels the colors of day
in a breath   and yawning, obliterates
difference with a dry salt breeze

Pearl pain
curled hand
she always, she never
colorless words
twisting to resolve

I did not know the light
I had inside

I did not know I could stop
to let it rise

Sun above, fire below, Popocatepetl—
our beginning called back in flashes—
rock   hardened by the hunger of the wind
black clay   smoothing distance
and closeness to the same contours.

Now, easy within the city's rush of color—
black silver white stream   light at the windows
encouraging.

The night sky of the country tells a different story—
the far visible   and therefore the smallness
of our planet and patch of earth
also visible   It is humbling to stand outside
and see the night sky with the naked eye.

She lived in a different country
   infamous winds
      blew the doors shut and carved streets bare

Direction came from outside
   common as north   south   disappearance and waiting

I did not know I had the breath of firelight.
I needed light   to capture the dark
I did it slowly   carefully
without knowing where it came from
or where the spreading touch of darkness would fold
to light again.

My senses came back to me   one by one
even as sightlessness poured from my eyes
and became a cry seeking lament.

Reblazing   breath opened a cavern.

And blood the one that kept track
   all blood
the beat of loss.

    VI. We

I brought her a knife she used to get away.

She took anything at hand.

When she wanted to save me,
I wanted to kill her.

I stabbed
        from inside to bring her down
gave the knife.

She wanted to save her life,
and kill the enemy by sacrifice.
Speed the credo, caring nothing about pain.

I wanted to be sacrifice, if need be,
slowly kill.

We both survived—
we

fierce,
twinned,
unforgiven mothers,
never named.

    VII. Story

Her stories were never mine
but I heard inside the stories
and I found another story, because that's what I do.

I heard the split   no one family—
sad girl with flat cheeks   unmoving mouth
alert to the disputed facts of her childhood
Unheld, she watched   hat snapped
under round chin   matching coat of woolen sorrow

She performed dislocation as leap
dance dizzying mid-air revenge
touching feet to the ground

She survived without knowing how to tell a simple story
but did not lie   There was chronology and conflict

Fantasy   a sacred text   passed on
        made of indecision and disappointment
                first and last, each day

She told truth in a rush
    hooked with questions, unresolved, and running to unanswerable
      for anyone who might care to know the ending
A listener perhaps

When does the listener become the teller?

I sought the truth without taking it in.
The hidden silence that was always there is there again, found—
I absorbed the loss
absorb
   the fear of loss

I emptied myself of all the circles including this one—
   it is hard to break a circle

I learned slowly
      to forget what I heard

I found my own story   by returning
to the beginning when everything mattered to me

I heard the ripples outward
   my hearing sense becoming my sight—
     just as one sense gives out, another recovers

Never mind—when speaking of the wind
   beginnings and endings
      have nowhere to go

When speaking of the wind
  I said, never mind
    beginnings, endings

Finally the story is
too large and must be made
from scraps   to do
it justice   no learning equal.

I return
to find my way
among the five directions—
to watch the sun sky
shadow of clouds like water
rolling in waves
across the ground.

Fire is faithful, she was made of air.

What bird of fire leaves the crust of the earth
smoking in skirts of lava?

Time to fly, a bird must rise.
I did not know it was my turn to go.

Your grief my grief

stricken open

until all the wounds are one

I have loved   You have loved

Is there anything else
delicate wounded one
difficult loved one

Watch out!
Explaining
skates to the edge

overlooks vast opportunity:
black ice   proud perfection—

once cut, leaves slashes
on the faces
underneath.

Twice

I came there twice
between the forms of beginning and the open end:

Once, looking in the mirror
  sinking past black pupils at last
   (I thought of cutting my wrists)
    to enter and remake the scream.

I felt entirely alone at 15.

Fear passed quickly, a shudder in my chest
but it was anger saved me   No!
through barbed white teeth.

No to the pupils free of the eye
turned inside to roam blue night
looking for a tinier window.

Don't give up!
(Life.)

Years later, I sat by the fire.
  I felt I had nothing left,
   nothing left to give   I saw it   despair.

  It was simple—two eyes facing the face
  empty.

Then, *this is not right* (even if it's true) and it could be true.
Another tick of the clock.
Enough.

I got up from the chair.

Cliff Face

I rode the bus   south to the City.
The last ridge took the light
    on its long stone flank   forest standing bare.

I should have known
    weeks before in Central Park:
        your naked face   paling
          as we walked together.   You stared
              past fervent grit-gray stone,
        iron sheet against the air:

    Strings of silken, dancing cord
        and soundless mirrors pasted
        on your cheek and brow
        fell from the cut of cold.

I decorated with floating words
    as if a nest could be made in flight—
        the dare and dance of birds.

I could not return
    and you turned inside a winter
where you saw no end but gray
        gnarled limbs curled in   curled round
a one-eyed cold, the familiar
leaving in the dark.

Conditions

1. If I am empty and emptier
   and no longer know
       how to weed out hollow fury
       how to walk away—cracked shell,
           rounded shoulder

   then the shape of a bowl is what I'm seeking
       space more than water
               air lighter than drifting sound.

2. If I cannot be hurt, then the wound was never forgiven.

   If I have learned to praise, then scars glow, old dry shiny moon.

3. I walk the hard dirt road

   slowly the flow of hillsides
   reach of trees
   across
   my shadow lengthening   curving
   I empty as I walk.

   One time, I saw a bull frog on the dirt
   big as a full-spread palm,
   brown skin peeled from one muscled thigh
   whole body in a pose of high alert
   organ spit out the back.

February Tilt

1. Cold ground, sharp grass—it was strange to feel so pinned down, alone.

   Paddlewheel of memory slapping water / sky: the frozen ground at eye
   level, mud in peaks, crystals lodged in cracks of earth and looking back
   at my small self floating over winter, no line of wing

2. A happiness came in the light
   I watched the sky become an orb

   the hollow beyond the trees like the hollow in the neck

3. Standing on the half-frozen ground
   as bird's wing carves a single shadow on the pond's ice oval

   Nothing to do with you   The slowness   slippery.

   Mud—one foot sunk and half the other.

Midnight Sun

How could it be after all this time: your scent on my wrist
not sweat   a cinnamon sweetness
at the base of my left thumb
indentation below brown flash and veins' rugged split

Was it the bright smell of morning rain,
                        or light streaming below the water's surface—
Above, below, bundling clouds,
                and at the end of the day: cicadas taking sunset
                                into rooms of sound.

I'd been thinking of the time in Norway
our midnight walks of birdsong and color
flowers turned out through the steady
ongoing blaze

and how I began to question you
   in the course of the bright nights
      without the shadow of any consequence
in the glare between us,

a focus on the distance. When we boarded ship,
I was sick and stayed in the cabin
until the medicine took effect.
I watched the wake of sun

go under in the waves.   Sunset grazed my hand as I slept,
only the sea faithful, never denying
the hours of the tide, the clock of the moon
as we rode south.

Translation

To fail is to admit I can do nothing more. Perhaps it's good. If I can fall, arms open, into the rhythm of it—letting the air pour through me, hands open—not the reason, closing hands—then failing is a passageway to the next right word.

I heard the words in the wind from the south and east and I ate them. That was how I translated the words delivered to me in a different language by your urgent tongue—we spoke and argued and you knelt and fingered the old Spanish dictionary from the 17th century. Curled in the library nook that saw the purple mountains and kept them at the bottom of every page every day, until their shape couldn't be seen anymore, the poems moving out, away from us.

The poem was a space for discovery and the translation—a world away—demanded accuracy and loyalty to the word, invented by holding a stranger's cup and drinking. An urgency that I had to touch—spit and thorny brush: I crossed worn sandstone on a trail at dusk.

Salvia Mexicana

Leaves curl together on the fur stem,
    purple bud and graying hood. White seed protrudes,
last punctuation of one life, ready
      to begin telling the next how to live.

Air burnishes flight from purple mouth,
    cold rain rumples the earth
      making the downward path easier
for all who follow: seed in the ground
  bound by mineral sands and fingertip moisture
of more rain, seeping wet and the new cold.

Everything inside the seed—needed, given.

Sage burns, sage blossoms—
    grows green, dusky, forgives this life,
      dries on the stalk, grows smoke.

Room by room, the air clears—
    the seed goes where there is no light.

desire lines (2020)

because ice is fragile.

the water rises and the water falls.

in winter how the water rises: arctic sea smoke, freezing salt spray, freezing mist (up and down)—and water falls: the evening rain turns to ice underfoot. first on the road, a sheen of black ice, faster than the thick crusted forms of white, gray spiral and bubbles.

the sound of rain is a rush in the veins after the changing slants
of winter.

i follow the sky now, never a line but altering skycap. the cloud, the trail, the storms from the north—nor'easters and the surprising pummeling from the southeast, a stormy organ.

the mark of air frozen under the surface: bubbles pooling flow in spirals, and the dust of snow on the surface. lines as white cap patterns, peaks to puffs, dotted stubble to dusted lines.

the face—lines on the face, re-meeting friends of thirty years ago, friends who stayed on. lines on the face, differently held. i froze or sweltered on subway platforms. they met the wind from the southeast when transplanting apple trees in march, harsh wind blast, boots half-sunk in mud.

i meet two at the farmer's market—her face emerges from behind a mask of lines as if she has faced into the wind all this time. she had a complexion smooth as a dolphin. the salt spray and orchards on the coast have changed her. the laugh is deeper. he looks the same, when he turns with the wooden box in his dark hands, pale green cardboard pints full of peaches. his rough face has held against the elements—rough, but kind.

late august, beautiful light. after moving to maine: i wake asking
myself in this gorgeous shell of light, what emptiness am i living in?
bones clattering, ground breathing so long and deep, i can't hear it.
i know that and wonder if i will start talking to trees again.
what the hell am i doing here? it's hard—not yet comfortable
inside the shapes of quiet that are so large.

summer. i swim out into the water, push off the edges. diving
deep, my limbs find full turnings. i roll beneath the motion
of the clouds. all august i swim. arrival and searching to place
memories in my new old place.

i meet m again. her father has alzheimer's, and she's going
through his papers. she's struggling to connect. he is not worried
about any of the papers. she feels terrible about throwing away
his things. she feels they are his memory. *she* has to decide what will be left.

we talk about not knowing what will be left, when it's our turn.
will it matter?

m's father worked with mies van der rohe in chicago after
getting his degree in architecture from nebraska and escaping
the camps, unlike the rest of his family who were interned
outside seattle during WWII. his brothers told him: leave the
university of washington. go as far east as you can to study and
get as far from the evacuation line as possible. as the line moved,
the internment of families required to register and be interned
expanded eastwards. he escaped by transferring to the university
of nebraska. he was ahead of the line.

mies van der rohe called his buildings "skin and bones" architecture. he strived towards an architecture with a minimal framework. structural order balanced against the implied freedom of free-flowing open space.

van der rohe asked m's father to stay in chicago and work with
him as he sought what he called a rational approach to guide
the creative process of architectural design. m's father wanted
a simple life in a smaller place and said no to being part of
van der rohe's chicago experiment.

m. grew up in madison, wisconsin where her father quietly
built houses.

today, m. is making clear lines on the black ice. she calls about
going skating and talking more. she is skating on the sudden
possibility brought by the deep cold. for two days, it is possible
to fly free across the ice on walker pond. i live here now, and
i am not ready to carve lines in the ice having just arrived on
the surface and still making prints in the snow. i need to feel
the downward collapse and support of snow. the give.

m. has talked to me about how great it is to have a conversation
on the ice, the sail off and return, skating side by side, then
moving away again across the surface trading stories. to know
when. shaped from what we expect in this winter place—
contraction and expansion and the wavering desire. we've been
talking papers and memory. how to sift someone else's,
to know when conditions are right. and how to sift, while moving
across the surface of the blank staring ice.

Uncollected Poems (1984-2023)

Oak, November
for Grace

There's an oak leaf, one   caught in the latch on the door
lodged like a letter in a letter box.
It knocks slowly, eight-prongs   the wind
tips it back, head leaning away   stem like a tail,
wind knocking softly   turning over the life of a tough brown leaf.
Stronger than a grasping hand, it takes years
for the veins to dissolve to brittle lace and still not want
to search the good brown dirt.
How did it? Why did it come so near the end? The oak.

From the bathroom window,
green rubber gloves across the sash
splay fingerless in crumpled, inside-out positions.
The leaf waves again.
The handsavers grow lazier and may have to go
in the trash bucket before the next cleaning.

I study the oak   the many kinds of brown
graying and reddening oak across the clearing.

The message will open, and I will not have touched the veins.

I write a friend whose blood is not making enough
more real blood   the kind that carries what we need
to every extremity in a day.   I spill out, too much on the page.
The oak scratches a life into the soft wind.

I wanted to send word, tell her I got the message—
you don't have forever you know.

Burying Winter
for Nora

The sound rang out
        as if the life itself (and everyone touched)
            became the sound
a bowl rung loud rung round, oh!
Grace herself ringing loud as the fierce life-loving sun.

A bowl, ready and clean
the song of empty
        sound rang out

A fire in the everyday belly of the sun
cried out a name

We heard it—and another, not yet known
the name of death as our own.

We could reach
outside of wild imagining
because of you

Living on

Nora heard it
    above the ground growing wide along the earth
        traces of fireburst in red salvia

moving through the full crown of leaves, sky's longer dark,
    frozen ground, dry cold and numbered shards of ice
            sound folding into lakebed bottom spring summer
days of sun and nourishing mud

Nora went rigid in the sun
all fluid tick-ticking
inside the marrow of her bones—
a chord played in her blood,
all given in preparation and given over on the day

whatever fiber

was left
unsounded, filled with sound

Pulled, kept moving
by forces outside
her,
by her own   children swimming
    in their grief   lonely bones up the hill   where Grace lived

Grief will not leave   urgent whispers greening
    The sound will not leave

Nora—
        her throat, a pitcher dry as bone
        pouring pain   no chord could play
the soundless song

The winter offered quiet at least
early dark   a burying winter
        so the sound could sleep
            in the bare sky
                be a naked branch
or cupping cold

Perhaps the sound will stay

A cloth can wipe the table
    four chairs   Pull up another
and winter can be buried without Grace

Blueprint

for Jane Cooper

    1.

I see a blue gray triangle
    filling the body's chambers
        breath across the collarbone   quiet down the ribs
            flowing flame at the solar plexus.
Peaceful
    discovery: breath drawn from the space of air outside the body
        penetrating tiniest nerve endings   clustered at the fingertips.

    Hear it   See it
        The sun reminds us of our time.

Peaceful curtain, drawing.
    Blue-gray inside orange finger flame.

    2.

A bird knows
    how to re-enter (an infinitude) the sky
        flying from the buildings   scaffold of wing.

Is the blue-gray triangle your mind
        growing rays from the cool hands of the clock
          towards a large still place:

Not supposed to live past the age of five,
on your own, you tuned in to adventure—
you wondered at what you saw:
porpoise signaling from the waves
or sleek plane carving space into shadow and sun.

Later, your poems tracked the sight lines
of aviators   clearing the bomb trail
and from the ground, "the sky... streaked with pilots falling."

Blue-gray porpoise, lasting, leaps into the sun.

Your mind skirts the universe   starlight from canyon floors
        and names far and near as blood   and stranger.

No use dying amid your sense
            of having to climb infinite ladders   and stay standing.

It will all fall down—the high cliffs beckon

                            The birds.

3.

Approaching the city
    from the west   I see the rising
        blue-gray towers, orbs, triangles,
            silhouette of mysterious Chrysler
        and Empire State buildings.
            The river strand shining white
                like your hair around your living
                    lined face.

I watched the cool slices of sky in the river current.

4.

It is the blue-gray, the changing cloudscape
    and the nest of orange sun behind the trees

Gray changes to rain   freshens the paved road.

    And when I ask, you direct me.
        I leave the door open a crack
            for higher heat—your mind aglow
                and three new pencils dreaming beside you.

Looking down, looking around for clues   I say little
"It's all so uncomprehensible," you reply

Your eyes, the blue-gray
                looking out from the horizon

Protections
for my father

1. I walked with him
   in bright February
   blue eyes bleared by cutting wind.

   He spoke carefully as usual
   but bare-headed, unheeding,
   the wind marked him—
   he who always wore a cap,
   a banded, short-brimmed hat,
   or beret, muffler at his neck.

   Ice-pocked sidewalks,
   he chose the middle of the street
   and we walked the length of Foster,
   dog-legged on Sparks, turned right to the hospital.

   How is it, all of a sudden,
   the bruisy tone
   of skin around the eyes
   not seeing as much as before
   and less to tell

   When will noticing stop
   and being be there alone?

2. In shock, he walked on the cold day
   to visit his wife, make plans to come home.
   He decided there and then
   he would be at home
   when his time came.

   There was a measure now
   even as he told me, his grown daughter,
   for the first time, how strange it felt:
   to feel pretty much the same inside
   but change so much that some days
   he didn't recognize himself in the mirror.
   Or to hear his wife say

after the diagnosis
that she needed 24 hours to be alone.

This Picture

You sent me to Mrs. Mac's wake
*to make an appearance, to represent
the family.* McCartney's Garage, founded by Hazel and Sewell
H. McCartney in Harvard Square. When he left to care for
her parents, she carried on, slipping under chasses
on a dolly in her deep-pocketed work coat with a blue collar.

What did you want me to see at the wake, what was it
really? Some preview of your own
dead white appearance–beaked nose breaking the sheets,
the day's light. Well, Mrs. Mac was there
with all of white Cambridge–beaked silhouette
and hair like a shock wave of broken
foam. I didn't need to see her
but I did need this picture:
how the dead become instant strangers
and the living make them up from there.
Flowers banded together like wheels,
I sign out, signing your name too, as if you had
made the appearance, your own disappearance becoming
more likely. As if we'd seen something together
that you knew I would be seeing,
would have to see, alone.

Chemistry
for David

1. Current

You don't wait
but leap into a boat
downshore,
rush by on the current
waving "Hurry, hurry"
as I run
along the shore
rocks   low brush   high grasses
trees overhang the river.
I leap through the blue-green landscape,
listen for my brother's call
and arrive at a knowledge
without destination.
Were we ever together
I wonder   never   now .

2. Cluster

He became an alarm
set off   running talk
dizzying the air. Open-
mouthed, my tongue
flat like an ear
willing myself
to be able to hear him,
catch his meaning,
anticipate, unravel: connect.
Impotent, the great clusters
hung in the air, but when words became music,
quiet found itself and me.
I walked away,
bright day in the wild
walking between
the trees, naming the scars
on the sides of the rocks
and what they had to say.

3. Magic Trick

"First the blindfold..."
I who believed
mirrors could be walked through
sideways... I would enter the thick dark
happy to be on the inside of surprise,
wrapped and unwrapped, just ahead.
He tied it tight, a big knot, no light —
just the home of my guessing brain,
and my unblinking brother trust—
all will be revealed—fear
turning like a fan,
under his sleight of hand.

"Time to remove the blindfold,"
he would intone, the secure unknown
soon to be unmasked.
Opening the quiet dark, mirror
like an open book,
I looked and looked
for any sign reflected in the unbandaged world.

Willing subject,
I did not see
he needed me
holding the bubbling tubes of charcoal
and smoky blues
glistening inside the glass
of his one-wall
chemistry closet home.

Same Time
for my mother

I saw the light fly by
gray-yellow in the dusty window slide.

My old memory
no longer all I remember
living:
       Spring
       become death-cut,
       open-ended wound.
       Rejection of the news.

Sun hits the north side
and creamy ovals rain
down blossoms:
       your arms
       the day
       around my neck,

       your life
       the pull
       against my chest.

I remember the petals riding down the Charles,
    your breathless forehead in closing sun,
        apple limbs unburdening in the river.

Furious blowing
    raining up up down,
not like the rain yesterday
    from nowhere—whole sky let go.

You too come back in light.

Three candles lit since morning
burn down in the sun.

My mother lately

My mother lately has smiled in my dreams,
and opened her hands for me to stop and read.
She breathes color into my small room,
praise.

And I am allowing her hard-pressed life
to rip the sewn-up seams and take her own sweet time:
No fire in the night or dread at the lip of basement stairs.
She is not waiting, cast to keep watch
by the door on the third floor
where her father died only weeks after
she was sent away.

Then I dreamt about Eva,

how she went stiff in a chair then fluid again,
a scare. Naomi was there.
It was all all right.

Eva didn't mind the suddenness, a few
seconds long. She was unsurprised.
As long as she returned, she said she didn't mind.

I felt her body before me,
I felt her go, sent through and back,
    the shock through flesh to bone, bone to breath—
I was the chair, outer frame.

She said calmly, that's the way it is
    and that's how it's going to be.
We're all in line   body bone flesh.
Be glad you're here and I held on.

Dear _____ ,
for Adrienne Rich

I thought (of you)   all the time
        how we carry the day, drag all of it
    with us in wet nets
along the studded rocky shore

Some look up   some don't   as they dig

    from the East
    fire   blackened, always at the edge of your eye
        and bell of night
      from Orion : and the One bright above in the Northeast
    the chunky brilliance
        flowing garment of the Milky Way
                partial palm print on my window

How you believed in the sky at the end, held the cracked
cracked brilliance in your bones   galaxies seeing from another   fearless eyehead
    unturning

Yesterday   honoring you, night seeker who loved
        trailing stars and hard ground
    the journey between: dream kept breaking, right up to the high-water mark
handsome sky ablaze down to the treetops   forehead with stark writing across
crabbed bones   becoming all bone and ready to heave it all
        off the edge   into the fire belt of stars

Banner
for Bob Nichols

1

Bob wore salvia in his blue shirt buttonhole,
brilliant summer lasting in Grace's garden: red as red can be.

2

Where Elsa lives: three beds of salvia, flaming ovals at the end of the drive
on the family dairy in the old stone house next to the barn.
She sells eggs, stacked in the deep doorway and vegetables on the card table
by the road, honor system. She laughs about her high beds of salvia—
how everyone comes up the drive to talk about them—
"You'd think there were no more flowers in the world."

3

A banner year for salvia and I kept thinking as the fall wore on, past Grace—
how she always watched the spaces between pulling to make room for every kind,
how the smaller buds miss her hand, zinnias popping heads and tough pale stems,
blue pansies curling to sun.

The vegetable garden just over the lip of the hill, tomatoes still coming, long squash,
and pumpkin, beans gone by, and Bob tramping by, walking slowly
looking up   at the curving line of trees
looking down   hands in pockets
at the thick flower tangle—the salvia upright
announcing triumph
because it knows death
alive   alive.

Neighbor
for Joyce

There's a cost to learning
how to be human
and who pays we don't know
until your own time turns certain.

The road between their place and mine
is a rutted lovely road. Every time
I wonder if I have the time
to bump the shocks and cross the road I love
or if I have the time to walk—

round the downward turn of high stone wall
that holds the meadow to the hill, past the sun cast
on the pond, blades of bright marsh grass spiking the gully,
a vista of strange comfort in the valley spreading to woods.

One spring day, my neighbor faced me
sun on her pale face and flicker-green eyes—
she said she needed to measure her time carefully
and didn't know how long.

When I saw the owl leave the glade
and pour its thick winged body deeper into the woods,
I remembered the need to nest in peace
and the urge of some to die in the quiet of the many trees.

Fado

for Tom

Some believe it's lucky to die.

I think Tom was like that,
                the way the door was always open
                                for whatever came, whatever showed up.

Not open-handed just open for business.

   He had a beauty to him, a clear-featured face,
                playful mouth, surprising laughter
sounding from his chest
                as he lifted his long black hair
                        from his back with a turn of the head.

How many times he walked unscathed from the beckoning curve
                where the Hancock crossroad t's?

   Was it a blue Sunbeam he wrapped around the tree,
                at last earning the name "Tom's corner"
as he walked, whistling, the remaining six miles down the Point.

I remember making marble paper together one day at Gray's—
                the seaweed gum floating in the tray
                        dark blue orbs moving on top of the rust-colored
                combed figure eights as we drew the paper across swirling worlds
                        picking up slow-moving grace.

   And after all those years of slow and crazy,
                crazy came from nowhere very fast
                        when an angry man plowed down the hill
looking for someone else, knife in hand, he couldn't get in upstairs—
                and found Tom at home in his apartment on the alley
                        reading in his chair, door open to a cool night.

I imagine Tom held the room in his own light for a moment,
        his quizical ice-blue eyes taking it all in
                and then releasing his life quickly
                        to the stranger in it.

Tom made you want to turn around and look
   to be sure you hadn't missed something—
      he was watching the way the water below keeps the oily colors afloat:
         the marbling flow, alive and changing
      under the startling blue and black-lashed eyes,
         looking up from the paper and back into the pool.

Determining: Charles Homer Haskins

The cane rack to the right of the door held the measure of his gait—the canes leaned against each other forming a rugged silhouette, a strange, climbing skeleton made of wooden bones. The rack held a collection of canes—some chest-high, some rounded like a closed wing pulled close to the body.

He hiked with a walking stick. In early photographs, mountains dominate he and his wife, a broad brimmed hat shades his fair complexion, red mustache. Curiosity pulled me to the canes to rattle the bones and to touch the handles. Taken up first by choice, alongside a bantering wit, then filling a steady need, as he leaned further, harder into the ground with every step.

They didn't knock against each other, the shapely sticks, but were always changing positions. Still some of the canes were a very familiar shape—simple curved handle, brown stained wood. One was thin, elegant, black, a small mushroom top, tightly fit, to mark occasions.

Another stands with a carefully notched handle, a bone grip in an undulating shape where the palm's wide fullness can rest, the fingers wrap and grip. A silver cap, a pointed tip, a dapper evening cane is not there among the assortment. But a feeling of remembering intrudes as a tall stick, thick, arm-pit height for a medium-size man. A carved grip, a hoary head, a beard, a goat, a deeper cut for the eyes blank intensity. Ivory, brown bark honed smooth then dropping away in folds like ledge, the handle meeting wood. Sturdy, forthright, all to balance the weight and measure of a man when the architecture of his skeleton fades and must alter its relation to all around him—like the mountainside and its fatal points of fissure, the slow dynamite of wind and inner storm splitting and melting the petals of stone.

And even a mountain goat, late in life, comes to a crevasse and must leap, scrabble up the other side to sky and air's tunnels, so when the time comes to leap without the same, sure-footed strength, there must be the clattering fall against the sides of stone, the old head cleaved and then airy, empty of all except the bones left strewn down the mountain.

I am still growing into my bones, when questions come blurting out of my mouth, the moment they occur to me: Whose canes are these? Whose canes are these?

Your grandfather's.

Never having seen them used or even touched, I reach for them, a young girl, curious about the echo into the unseen chamber of the past. The house he criss-crossed, the streets he walked. Whose life is here? Curiosity blooming from the touch of his palm on wood, bone. They belong to him.

I inspect the shapes, feel the different woods, hand sliding over his canes. There is a sound that is not clatter but a deep wood ring, when the canes knock the square rack. The canes are strong, stronger than bone and without flesh. He is the same—no person here—but his pace is traceable through the steps made easier, burden taken and borne by the canes. They help steer him through the hours of the day, they help the body navigate a wider possibility. The eastern light around the door into the hallway— brightens the wall where the canes face north into the deep hollows cast onto the white background. Quiet lightning casts like thought from the air out over the mountain. For over forty years, the canes stayed in the hallway, determining time.

I follow his gait out the door, listen for the odd music pulled from the bones. The Parkinson's turned him rigid, even as he toed the edges of the crags, staring at the air currents that served the falcon and cut the stone, the goat unmoving, until the wind alone could take him down.

In a dream, my grandmother shows me the room where my grandfather died:
The bed is empty, sheets wrinkled from many hours of weighted sleep, the mark of a cacoon-like body, wrapping itself tighter and tighter, until ironbound, there was no air, just the tremor of breath.

Bright air and hard mountain.
I find the rhythm of thought and his motion through the world.

The Monarch butterfly, rust and black, flies thousands of miles to return.

Daylight stunned in purpling tongues,

sunset swallowed by hurricane winds,
the sky signs over the sea below

Right hand slides like a spreading rooftop
        sputter of nerves writing to darkening daylight
yielding to rain

Wind whip down the spine of the city
flogs the back alleys to fetid strips
as jackets, shoes and twisted pants
rise and bang in slurry motion
against the iron gates and archways

Turn back
clutching to gutters, attic portals,
half-beams sagging under rooftops.
while others freeze half up the staircase
and waters lap at clean, bare ankles.

Many years since the river flowed before deeper, held secrets,
now sluiced along a concrete runway straight to the Gulf.

How long
    to wash away the milky silt
        that covers the bottom of the river like an old tongue
            sponging up everything the land has to give
                holding tiny root hairs
                    together, apart

Growing tendrils that suck nutritious swamp brew
    and pull fresh water from the brine.

The crowd of 200 founded an island
on the cement skirt outside the Astrodome
They lifted the new-formed community off the pavement
and began to cross   young and old stretched   across the empty freeway
pushing wheelchairs   in determined knots, young held high,

to reach high ground.
They moved together and snaked across the bridge
    spanning a two-mile hump of freeway leading out of the city
        to meet the promise of rescue.

They believed The Good News sworn over a loud speaker outside the dome.
They believed the buses were coming—hurray!— to the freeway to carry them to safety.
These 200 marched right into the law—the Sheriff and his manned blue wall
come from the other side of the river to say, No,
This is no New Orleans and never will be!

The blue wall, 3-man-deep
held against them, citizens of the empty freeway
who marched out of the flood seeking
not to die.

Together, they fled again, a story of surviving,
back towards the city's swirling drain.
They stayed dry,
camped under an overpass.
They made a toilet out of a storm drain and teens
rigged a privacy curtain from bike wheels and scraps of plastic, until
their encampment's shield was busted up
by the backdraft of helicopters sent to disperse this unseemly ring
of New Orleans citizens who invented shelter and shared food.

When law enforcement's guns came out,
groups of 8 hid out in stringy knots,
holding onto water's rising rot,
the stuff islands are made of...
heads ducked below the line of windows
and above the line of water
hiding under the seats in an abandoned
school bus.

The mouth of the river   torn speechless
what news
    toothless music...

In the day, shipping to the world's ports,
    open waterways took in more traffic, freighters
        crowded the sunken hipped harbor,

gouged deeper, wider.

Many years since the waves rocked the barrier islands,
cradle to the Mississippi, buried in a run-off ditch.

Rancor   a ribbed boat cage
   captained by the face of sour regret
      expects to come ashore

      to steer from madness to peace

as if there are two shores and a choice.

How unhappiness
hurts, then roots along a changing shore
dangling threads in the darkness of solitary weeping.

Destruction has no vocabulary
but birds fleeing fled the wind   days before falling from the sky
onto the Plains in droves.

Do not be afraid—
the synapses will return.

Coffee bananas   held in port grain ready and readying
   to ship from the heartland
      the largest shipments of the year, clogging the Mississippi
the traipsing nerve   a river flailing mud fire corpses
and inside the city, elders in sundresses, face down in the water.
Grandmothers floating by, slippered and barefoot.

The river blocked, unable to disgorge its grain.

Emergency shelter at The Superdome, unable to disgorge the dead.

Entrance stopped. Exits blocked. See a man in his deck chair, hat on,
cotton plaid short-sleeve shirt, expired in the heat.

The hand let go   hard to hold the hand   of earth being torn from her roots.

Death's door knocking.

The mouth of the Mississippi
        a water moccasin
            undulating olive brown snake, dark cross bars shiny with oil
                    seeking cooler waters through gassy rainbows
    urging a path away from the burning heat, night and day
            burning   water ash burning   waterbirds gone
                water blistered trunks
                            and high elms of the city
            shedding brown leaves in shivers like a snake turning in the sky
and falling on death's table
of water.

i was reading truong in April

and it was colder inside and warmer outside, growing warmer in the minutes left/ April
sun—3 minutes more daylight/ the plastic sun porch, a roaring oven by 2/ when i open
the doors to the inside and let the rush of heat set the ceiling fan in motion/ so it's an
early morning here—the hot cold april: how can it be so cold, so still,

the quality like a well, a plunge into sadness,
the ground releasing, cold moistening the old
oak leaves' cover, sun pulling the pores,
of the small 2-room house where i sit on the earth,
not far from the gray rock outcrop
where the room fills with blue—

the sadness, a throat
as i read truong's
book. i hear the heat
of hot stones dropped
into the well
        and i count the number of times he finds
for the word: whisper
   knowing it is the sound of the hot stone
      finding black water in the earth.

a tongue. his. it's one
you've never heard before.

In the dry well of the afternoon,

she answered No
she didn't want to add anything
about getting an education
in prison—what it meant.
She sat right on the corner
of the two tables pushed together
crowded with women in green.
Later, her head rose even higher—
gazelle at the edge of the grasses
long neck arched, chin tucked in
listening hard
for the sound of approach.
They don't want us to learn, she said
her head turns a quarter turn, freezes.
They mock us—the guards—
they do everything they can
to undermine us.
Quick intake of breath,
the snap of fire taking hold
in the updraft
of silence
surrounding her.

Falling
for Ada Gates
and for Doris Eddy

1.

A shot in the open field, the mare shies under me
streaming sideways   I lean against

the center of gravity: her long dappled
shoulders whitewater over her bones.

My knees fold and unfold
like wings against the dark leather.

She rears up, I cover my face
as I fall   flags of light   reins loose in my hands.

2.

The mare returns to her stall, her
dappled coat dotted with indigo, the liniment
and salve for her wounds

that never heal   the ropes that tie her
keep her steady on her feet
far away from the milky walls.

She has splintered two stalls
kicking steady as a mule and paws
the floor bald in a few hours, neatly

squaring all the hay behind her
outside the need for four walls
outside her high sensate head.

Her taste instead is for space and she chews
the wood to tufts around the latches'
glinty screwed-in stubs.

Let out, she runs

over fences, just mended, over ground, just dug
over her shadow rippling under her hooves.

    3.

I wake sitting up—raw
current sprints my spine.
Afloat on my bed, sheets thrown back,
she flies by the open window,

a trail of tiny bubbles blurring
the glass   She's out.
I run to meet her, spastic swimmer
through the doors   pawing at the openings.

The cold mud seeps back in   quick
impression of her hooves smoothed over.
I listen for the return of hoofbeats.
We stand off—a steady arm raised

follows the mare as she looms
in and out of the trees
We run to track her, not to catch her.
She will fall and we are running short of breath.

The front yard mud sends her down
thrashing heavy on the ground.
Talking low to the mare's deaf dread,
we pull the knot around her neck.

She is listening to everything outside this night
the holes   where her hooves have been.
Her eyes film the drowned birds
of her life, surfacing

in her dapples.
Her nostrils deepen red–thin coat of blood
bubbles with her breath. Our hands rise up to touch
the mare whose chest is heaving.

We fall away, fence fear from ourselves,
as she softens after a shot, and learns again

to stand, lumber back
into her remaining walled life.

Dear Half,

I feel the unwound
             cave heart
  that does not speak
    but guards a well.

Blood something.

On the Bus

This stranger seemed new to the world—chalky skin, so very pale, dusky brown hair, fine but thick, dry, unnourished and tired. Large, pale blue eyes, a Roman nose in a long-jawed face—jutted chin, teeth gone, so his skin falls around the mouth's long line. New, brown short-sleeved shirt and pants—black canvas shoes with a thin white sole—bright white—more like slippers than shoes. He stands in the aisle of the bus, he was once a tower, and he bags and re-bags, ties and unties his three plastic double-bagged pouches. One's for cans. He asks politely across the aisle for the discarded soda can—bags it, nestles the three bags in a different order in the rack above.

The rain starts and the wipers swipe the large windshield clear. He pulls a cotton T-shirt from the green canvas bag on the seat beside him and wraps his head expertly, one knot in back, the sides falling to shoulder length. He's ready for the rain. He announces he's going to Lynchburg, when he thanks the young man, a handsome Mexican, alert to his own good looks, blue shades, gelled hair and a goatee. The blonde Southern co-ed just in front of the tall stranger began working on the younger man from the moment he turned his profile to her. His answers are careful at first—two words—but when he gets off for the 10-minute rest stop, she follows. They stand smoking and laughing, and when they get back on, they move to sit together. Just when they enter a private whispering, the man in the soft-slippered shoes, speaks up—used to talking without anyone listening. "Excuse me," he says too loud, "Don't mean to bother you, but I want you to know I appreciate the can. I've just been released from the Department of Corrections. I can get the deposit, and I'm a need every one I can get."

"Sure, no problem," the young man smooths the air with his blue reflector glasses. The man continually shifts the three bags in his hands, then gestures with a large palm, the flesh both old and young, loosely knit to the long bones. He leans into the aisle speaking to the young blonde with the black bra visible under her oversize T-shirt—" You live in Lynchburg?" "No," she says, "I wouldn't live there. It's WAY too small." Leaning on the words, so he'll know there will be no further conversation as far as she's concerned. What would be the point? She checks her cell phone the way some people used to play with a cigarette—studying the ember, flicking the growing ash away, taking a draw and blowing a steady stream as if trouble could be blown away. She flicks the phone open, shuts it with her thumb, caresses the case against her face. The young man leans in, whispers into her ear, into her neck. She smiles, looks down, flips open her phone, and takes a call, answering back and forth easily Spanish to English.

The Tower stands, moves all his bags with him down the aisle, then returns with a brown paper sack he stashed further along. He hauls out a Hero sandwich, eats it with a private hunger. He has a one-way ticket to Lynchburg, Virginia where he could get help.

They'd look him over, maybe set him up by the end of the week. He knew the look, didn't know if it mattered about looking back. There'd be a chance. They'd decide there and then whether to help him or not. He needed help on the forms, someone who wouldn't mind his questions. He didn't know what his chances were.

He felt tired suddenly looking at all the new faces on the bus. He was greedy for them, and still saw all the others—Ommie, Ray, Tickleberry, Duane and Jolly. His best friends, all in his head—but he was surprised by who blinked in, blinked out, faces he thought he'd want to forget.

He tried to imagine everyone in the bus filling out forms. The sun cut across his lap as the bus swooped into Charlottesville. He cranes his neck to see the different way the shadows fall, bold in the city. Large, glassed-in buildings, banks and offices, lots of work here, but the way everything's on top of everything else and windows like the boy's reflector glasses, a person could lose their own shadow here. Seeing on all sides is alot of work from the bus.

Inside, they called him the Lighthouse, because he rose above 'the sea of humanity' they said—tall, white and always looking around, turning his head to watch the movement of the others—how something would start and ripple like the wind through the men—a circle would open, a tiny storm, fast, bloody—then disappear below the surface, someone left on the ground.

He called the guards "The Wind," and he made up signals to show which way the wind was blowing. At the exit interview, they told him some things would be different. He didn't know where he'd be sleeping by the end of the week, but he knew he'd walk all around town to see things for himself. It was okay with him to land in a smaller place—he just hoped they had his shoe size. They told him it would be ok to say that he'd just been released.

The bus was going on, all the way to New Orleans hitting town in the evening of the last day of August. He'd take his chances in Lynchburg. There was talk about a storm coming to the Gulf. He looked around again and tried to see about where each person was at. They used to joke inside: The Lighthouse never sleeps.

"Lynchburg coming up, be sure and pick up all your belongings." He had his plastic bags hung from his left hand, the canvas bag at his feet. He'd like to stay on to New Orleans, ride out a storm—just once, to be in the center of something big. Turn off the light sweeping in circles from the center of his forehead warning everyone for miles around. Just blink the damn thing off. Pull out the wires. Fuck the rest of them. He was tired. He wanted to close his eyes, he thought, as he ducked his head to leave the bus. His long legs unfolded before him as he stepped onto the pavement and felt the heat burn up through the flimsy soles.

Today, I hear how the old woman asks

for pliers from the pawnshop owner
to pull her gold teeth, pawn them
and pay her electric bill.
He refuses—tells her No,
don't come back,
gives the words their currency.

The Last Postmistress

As of January, they don't want a Postmistress—it'll be all PSE's.
Part-time, no benefits for them to worry about that way.
I have until 2014 to find another Post Office, at which time, if no luck,
my benefits are cut and I'm out of a job. But that's nothing: I know a man
who was told last week that his Post Office would be shut by February,
and he'd be re-assigned in the State of Maine, but it could be anywhere.

If he says, No, tough shit. Meanwhile, he may or may not be moving he doesn't know
  where
at the end of January, time's ice fishing begun, and his home not saleable at any price.
Here, the hours will be cut to six. They'll hold a town meeting to see
what they want to do, what hours they want to be open and when they
want to be done by. Earlier would be good, suit the work best, but it's out of my
  hands.
Senator Collins wasn't able to do much with the rest of them. I'd like to tell them to go
  fuck

themselves, sons a bitches, before it's too late, but with our luck,
they'll figure a way to make the paper the money's printed on dissolve somewhere
in outer space. Imagine. Like to call it a cloud. And what's a man or a woman
to do with that? When every form of speech is taken, and decent work too, make nice
and let them shred our union contract. I wouldn't mind being cut back some, if that's
  all they
wanted from me. They will only do worse, you wait and see.

They'll be the ones left counting up "the losses," and as for you and me,
once we go, when we didn't rightfully have to, the door's open, the deal struck.
And they can just keep whittling away, until we are left with nothing and they
are their own kings. Can't blame the union, they done the best they're
able, given the Congress refusing to allow any change in the terms or ease
our paying ahead 70 years on the Health Benefits pension, the one we won't be alive to
  see in our hands.

So what's left for us to hold tight to, ask and in fairness, demand?
What can we say where we're facing unsure shelter, no job or free
time to look into it all? Doesn't take a genius... Downturned and quiet, it's all in the
  eyes—
where high expectation goes when at every turn, it's blocked,
and hope pushed down by unlawful consequence, unbidden, pulled from the air,

and invented to sap the confidence and bright anger of how can they

do that! Sands of time couldn't be worth much, when we pay ahead to thicken the pot
    those guys
are planning to rob. At the least, let every postal worker, woman and man, dare
to strike between the eyes by saying what they want before the whole thing goes bust.

The way of stamp, handwritten envelope, weekly pay stub and slick-printed prize
is not anywhere to be seen, nor tender-eyed new year's luck.
No one day can revise the slow slip of February, and the ice-cruel story of our last
    Postmistress.

Dangerous Letter(s)

1.

Dear _____ ,

I'm done expanding
     to take it all in
The spindle crown aflame with wind,
     the arcing limbs blow and bend
I wrack and cough from my stiff-ribbed bed,
hope for calm smooth dreams

Trees understand the air worship where they are
They blow and bend take it all in   Later, bloom.

2.

How could you say nothing

How could you say when

How could you imagine

How could you tell
I was sick and coughing
the full lung tree red

What a storm we had, dear

I had almost forgotten what it felt like
  to expel illusion, breathe free

Clear sweet help
at the edge of the wood, soft brown
beech leaves cling
cling until they whiten and their fine ribs despair

The rest is moving fast faster without us:
  short day, long night, the dark dear

dear _____ ,

so much to say to the empty
love, to the tight-skinned, leafless beech tree.

The View from Pisgah
for Arthur & David

I left my half-glasses in the Pisgah State Forest
slipped from the side of my midnight
blue vest growing colder all night
inside the outline
magnifying:

It seemed right   my having turned 50   the three of us together
as the light pulled down into the earth
after our circular walk through the woods on Hallowe'en.
We could just make out the duskiness   our aging features, the gray purple
 trees and blueing shapes between   sponging up what was left.

I'd heard that day on the radio about the origin of bones in bonfire—
how the cattle were herded through the smoke-laden air of big fires.
The insects would be killed off before they moved
into close quarters for the winter.
I take a stick in my hand   study the blade like the curve
at the back of the shoulder   to feel the relation between my arms
to retrieve the fire between: image of the bonefire.

Next day, I go alone to retrieve my glasses just where I thought:
climb the further rise in midday sun
run my hands through the mat of grass and milkweed hulls
hold the pods up to the breeze to watch the flight of seed heads fly
then bury their ticking hearts under pine beside the old tree graves.

I lie back down   unwilling to leave the sky
of sudden perfect blue warmth
the taste of infinity like ascending
milkweed's dark brown dots.
Is this what my glasses stored in the night?

I close my eyes:
muskrat, fox, dog and deer,
gopher, possum, mink and crow,
otter, oxen, big-horned sheep,
eyes gold, brown, green,
striped and staring
as if the hill itself recites

the feeding, nesting, hunting
paths of all who've come.

The record stands
in the bright warm day as the animals sniff and snort
move through the rise   the red black brown marrow
the rotting earth   the walking backs of mountains.

The Card, the Note, the Envelope
for Ellen G. D'Oench

1. I had the card, a Samuel Palmer painting, that you and your father
    loved—"The Magic Apple Tree," circa 1830. Brown ink,
    watercolor, gouache and gum arabic. Modest among the work
    you knew, it was rough-hewn, a glowing gold
    meadow heaped in light behind apple orchard blasting
    loaded, drooping gnarly limbs over sheep and shepherd
    on curving path that tunneled through the valley to some darker envelope
    of lasting green and shade.

2. I could not send the note—could not.
    I did not want to make beautiful words
    on a card—the chosen stamps:1954, Brown vs Board of Education,
    and Navaho turquoise necklace to make up the new rate—
    to close and name a circle.

3. It was not a circle.
    It was broken, raw
    breath and breathing
    choked,
    the unbroken will
    angry laying in the bed
    ("Could we just do this?").
    You were in the last days—
    I had heard enough.

4. I prayed that you would not feel
    alone, afraid.
    I took the card, stamped, to write and send.
    I thought it might bring you some pleasure,
    a visual tie and bond,
    the color of time in hay-head's heap,
    but I resisted writing
    as if last dark/light could be stayed.
    And I knew you would know that
    being your self—
    how could I lie?

5. It was time
   you yourself named it.
   I decided it would be foolish to try and write,
   nothing could be right, except your own moments
   dropping, ragged,
   alive.
   It wasn't pretty or blank
   but peace rode out a full day's sleep. The white envelope
   unaddressed and unclosed.
   Nor have I looked inside
   to remember the desire to lift
   with words the floating veil of petalled shadows
   mottling the room, and covering your chest,
   until no breathing vined upwards.

6. I could send it now
   silent note
   and remember
   when I said I would visit on the Saturday, the day after you died, you said:

   "I'll write it down."

The Verge
on 2/3/13 for M.

It snowed the night
   white and black
And you are sharp
   outline of this tender visible
   seeing

This morning, every branch speaks to the air
   as it shades the ground

February: an ungallant, undeniable
     between

This is the juice, the squeeze between,
the time ground works
to bring round what we will know
and recognize—

How we need the verge

Caution Shoulder Work Ahead
Ice jam at the bridge Stream's locked
Busting concrete's cracking from the beam

I hear delirium, the changing blood
Water caught hard
Ungallant, undeniable
The water must through!

It could be called delirium
    speaking to many
     But it's not

Change

Layover

The horse's name was Kansas, one milky eye,
thickened winter coat. No halter, we stood
together in the open ring,
not an arm's length apart.
She stood, I stood.

I let myself be a person
in my bones, two-legged, thickened flesh at my hips—
feet, still agile, hands ready.
I did not move.

So you just want to be here, I said aloud,
Me too.
We stood.
I let her enter my body by standing next to her
and she grazed along my tiredness, my small fear,
and I let them spool into the ankle-high brown dirt.

Penny had gone to get hay
out of the car and check on the dogs,
roaming the muddy paddocks, suspiciously
quiet. I stood with Kansas.

She lowers her head and brushes me, knee to navel
with her long nose, twice, gently.
I reach for her powder gray neck,
open my hand—stunning softness and thick
bow muscle underneath her coat.
So strong. So soft, I say to her.

She reaches her head to nudge my hips.
You want me to get on—ride again?
I can't. It's been too long. And I hear the strangeness
of a disappearing path. Is it really too late—
for how many things?

I turn to her—OK. You want to walk, let's walk.
I start, the way Penny did,
Kansas on my right, walking in front of her left shoulder.

She follows. We do some loopy diagonals
and wobbly figure eight's.

I walk, she follows
but she knows she is leading the way, satisfied.
Ring time evaporates into the night air.
We walk together. All is right.
How long has it been?
Time wobbles in the figure eight
altering the circle.
We're cutting corners
making x's.

Why was I afraid,
and how has this become the shape of things?
I could walk a long time,
keep walking with this horse,
without ever getting on her back.
I could remember strong bones
in a ring deep in brown dust.

We walk to the half-gate.
I call out to Penny. No answer.
The purple webbed halter hangs above
on a nail. Kansas waits for it.
She nods her head.
I take it down, study the shape,
think I can remember.
I turn the straps top,
the open bottom, hold it to her
and she slips her head in.
We're ready.

I call to Penny
outside—three times,
then she comes in with a sack,
a collie at her heels.
Bring her over.

We walk by the other horses, some lit by a bulb,
many dark in their stalls, and I wonder
if they feel secure, safe in their stalls,
and how they hear distance, closeness, the dark.

Penny snaps a lead to Kansas' halter
and she pushes Penny with her broad skull
directing the next brush stroke.
Penny's hair falls in her face—
All right, all right, we're just slow.

She wags her gray head at Kansas,
and I lift mine higher to see the swirls
of sweat caked on the mare's back.
I go against the grain
to curry loose the dirt.

For Orlando: Make Beautiful in Maine

The mother sees her son's boyfriend on a stretcher being taken from the club, and she is afraid. *I knew*—gay club—when I heard it on the radio. Florida: old mistress to the Right, corrupt, stolen-election, multi-lingual, and one of the gay capitals. All at once.

It's happening all at once.

Sunday: called Hallowell friend (first open lesbian rep in the legislature) who told me another story: her 93-year-old mother insisting on reading *Becoming Nicole* aloud together, excitedly trading back and forth all weekend. And how in their family's church in Massachusetts the week before, the woman minister had welcomed C, a transgender 11-year old, to the service and suggested that the congregation might want to compliment C on her pretty dress as her two mothers, one a lesbian who had struggled with getting legal, proudly beamed on. So she retold the stories
and I remembered, we remembered
so many others, and yes, I have been shot with a deadly weapon,
thirty-five years ago, in bed with my lover, no hate crime name to it.

And most on my mind, how to stand beside my gender queer young, so they know that we can stand up, that it's all worth fighting and no, I did not say fighting *for*, because we don't need to say that. Maybe you do, but we do not.
We are. We make our love from what we are, from what is ours. Love and make beautiful, no matter what.

And before the Candlelight Vigil in Bar Harbor on Monday (having decided I was not going to go be inside a church or go to any inter-faith service without Muslims, Hindus, or almost any Jews), I woke up, my face numb. Hand to cheek, a casual gesture, face numb to my palm. Wanna call it PTSD? Never mind, I was messed up. No focus, no end of semester reports today—nothing to say.

I cried into the gash. Tears on my cheeks, neck. Today, teaching was about taking care and reaching out, because I was feeling desperate and tracking in circles like an animal caught alone in a trap. I understood eating your legs off to get out.

Messages: I write J and B, subject line: holding you. I force myself to go to a friend's photography opening, loved the burned sepia fog, the bleeding edges. That was Sunday, days ajumble. The thousand-year week. I go to the shore, white caps, face numb against the NW wind, no getting used to it.

Monday: Mantra today, Beauty is not enough! Beauty not enough!

J, hard not to be devastated by the hatred ...

Z, wanna come over?

It's hard to say that I haven't heard from anyone in my blood family.

Looking for company to go to Bar Harbor Vigil outside on the Green.

Tuesday: I need a three-day walk—I remember a very tall Native American in NYC after 9/11, and I mean the morning after, saying that Indians walk when they need to sort things out and that he walked with everyone, all the businessmen with briefcases, workers, secretaries in sneakers, everyone walking, walking, walking uptown on 9/11 and feeling all right, because everyone was walking together.

I was reading poetry for Astraea's Lesbian Writers Fund on 9/11. And we went—my Domestic Partner, Mexican/Jewish lover and I—to the women artists silent flash demo in Times Square. *Do Not Turn Our Grief Into A Cry for War!* A few days later, I read with another lesbian poet who now lives in Paris at the NYPL Amsterdam branch, and we read our own work and poems from the world, in translation. Today, the three-day walk is not happening—but I had three hours in the moss-shelved granite, pine forest of Acadia with my Maine childhood friend. That let me breathe.

On the way to the forest in Acadia, I saw flags at half-mast in Blue Hill, Ellsworth and at the Bagaduce Lunch! the clam shack a mile and a half from my house where the proprietor, cigarette in hand, once threw a group of us dykes off the picnic area in the 70's, saying I don't want people like you here. His offspring feel differently.

And outside the failed megachurch in town, the giant American flag is hauled right up to the top. I want to stop and ask a good Christian why the flag is not lowered. I want to go get a new electric chainsaw just down the Bar Harbor Rd in Trenton at Ellsworth Chainsaw—I need one anyway, a light hand-held re-chargeable saw, to cut the flagpole down, and its two smaller twin offspring, also. Cut them down. And I remember how a Penobscot dyke built her entire house with a chainsaw and asked the brothers over for an afternoon to get the ridge pole in place, and that was it. She built the whole thing— two stories—with a chainsaw, no problem. Or the women's retreat, built by chainsaw dykes and women carpenters, all the buildings hidden in the woods.

Everything's a long story now, unless I just start screaming like R last night,
Over 40 fucking years!
I'm getting behind now. I have to keep up with the news.

I really wanted to go into the failed Christian megachurch and be face to face, as close as

I could get, spitting distance, and talk about this. Words cutting sharp as chainsaw teeth, sharp as I could make them, to one of the people from the Christian Right club that sponsored over 200 bills against lgbtq people this year says Democracy Now.

Is there a problem? before revving up the brand spanking new chainsaw.

R said I always wanted to light that motherfucking giant flag on fire by the megachurch.

Then at dusk,
on the town green, the tall, young Passamaquoddy G sang a funeral song from his tribe, and three queers read 49 names in broken and strong voice into the dusk in candlelight. The air itself was tender. Candles going out, re-lit, held in cupped palms.

Driving home from Bar Harbor, I hit a deer.
Six feet to stop. Hauled the wheel left, right.
I looked right into the eye of the deer, head silhouette level with my sight line. *Live!* pounding in my bones as she flew through the air across the road and onto firm mown grass. She did not go under the car, but flew. I turned around. No sign of the deer. She flew. Her urgent bones leapt from the threat. I know what that's like. Then she disappeared.

So strange, one human family, O said. Unintentional harm to the deer; and intended harm, the shooter planning murder. Same human family.
Empty hurt.

The deer flew.
My bones run ahead of me, cannot settle.
Angry.

I am angry—the young queer spoke last at the Vigil Monday, and this, right after the first Gay Pride Weekend *ever* in Bar Harbor. Tonight, blue hair, green streaked and half-head shaved, queers under the gazebo on the Town Green squinched close together on the railings, calves tattooed, lighting, re-lighting candles for the dead and wounded. Tending flames. Wind from the northwest, murder from the southeast.

And at the end of the week, I tell my cool acupuncturist that I feel threatened, and she wants to know if something happened. I cannot tell her, It's everyday
in the thousand year week. We live, survive and love because.
I try to explain, I've been shot before. It brings it all up.

Many dead before this, I'm not alone.

Tuesday morning: I wake angry.

How to be with my lgbtq people.
I want equal protection without getting married.

Home from the Vigil, images of young lgbt kids in South Korea sobbing.
Deep, comforting. We can stand up, we have before...
There are things to do: Learn Spanish better. Be kind for no reason.
And there are some things I will not do: if anyone tells me we are all the same,
I will tell them, No, No es verdad!

And in the footsteps of queer elders here in Maine, I planted dark red dahlia tubers
today on the last day of the week of a thousand years when 49 died
and I will wait for the fall
bloom of blood blossoms
braving the edge of more cold.

Wind's split octaves

explain why I hear my heart
in the tree's leaves—poplar's water shiver,
large-palmed maples, iron-spun brown oak.

Sometimes, the wind reaches so far inside,
leaving nothing unturned, I find myself
welcoming an intimate chat with my stray selfishness.
Acting as if, a ventriloquist, I feel my mouth open and close
just to let the air sweep in
and out comes a giddy howl of laughter
stirring blood to my cheeks.

Arrow leaf falls
sharp, angry among the others
and wind comes, covers the ground,
sends up loneliness
helpless against itself.
Wind leaves love
among the ruined.

Sun passes into tree,
copper sheath, birch bark white
grows a house within a house,
roof of shining leaves.

Acknowledgments & Notes

I am grateful for the insight and care of Jan Clausen, Elena Georgiou, Rosa Lane, Olga Lange and Roz Parr in assembling this collection. Thanks to THERA Books publisher Donnelle McGee for his commitment to the work, to Mona Z. Kraculdy for book design and THERA Books Assistant Editor, Colleen Mills. I extend sincere thanks to Ellen Driscoll for permission to reproduce her stunning artwork on the cover.

Deep gratitude to my earliest teacher and poetry companion, Jean Valentine.
And sincere thanks to those who came as gifts in my life, a bit later—
Jane Cooper; Grace Paley; Eva Kollisch & Naomi Replansky; and Marie Ponsot.

Thanks to many for their support of my poetry in the years of writing and publishing these collections, including those passed, and those still present: my brother David Edgerley Gates, and my parents, David and Clare Gates; Electa Arenal & family; Margot Balboni; Kyle Bass; L.R. Berger; Celia Bland; Lee Briccetti; Brenda Buchanan & Diane Kenty; Lynnsey Carroll; Leslie Chatterton & Allyson Ford; Betsy Crowell; Eric Darton; Daphne Dejanikus & Julian Simon; Anna Dembska & Andrea Hawks; Brendan Doyle; Cornelius Eady; Carl Elsaesser; Louise Fishman; Catherine Francis; Gates family—Ada; Bob; Puffin, Dodie & Paul; Katharine & Ted; Peter & Joan; and Will; Lucille Goodman & Patsy Rogers; Marilyn Hacker; Victoria Hallerman; Peter Harris; Catherine Haskins & Jane Nilson; Scott Hightower; Fanny Howe; Helen Howe Braider & Chris Braider; Bert Hunter; Judith Jerome & Linda Nelson; Mia Kanazawa; Bhanu Kapil; Ron King; Bea Kreloff; Tony Kushner; Joan Larkin; David & Carole Larson; Jan Heller Levi & Christoph Keller; Helena Lipstadt; Becket Logan; Thomas Lux; Heather McHugh; Sandra McPherson; Jaime Manrique; John Masterson; Cassandra Medley; Jay Meek; Leslie Middleton & Patrick Punch; Cathleen Miller; Bob Nichols; Carol O'Donnell; Diana O'Hehir & Mel Fiske; Sharon Olds; Nora Paley; Roz Parr & Charlotte Abbott; Em Peake; Robert Penn; Sarah Petit; Monique Ponsot; Martha Ramsey; Alastair Reid; Bessy Reyna & Susan Holmes; Mariana Romo Carmona; Sonia Ragir & Sal Tagliarino; Leslie Ross & Zeke Finkelstein; Assotto Saint; Marianne Schretzman; Mitchell Sendrowitz; Vita Shapiro; lee sharkey; Barbara Smith; Juliana Spahr; Karin Spitfire; Matt Tannenbaum; truong tran; Arthur Tuttle; Chuck Wachtel & Jocelyn Lieu.

Gratitude for ongoing support & inspiration from the creative community formed in the Vermont and Port Townsend, Washington MFA experience.

Thanks for support from A Different Light Bookstore and NYC lgbtq community; the Sarah Lawrence MFA circle; Hardscrabble Hill, lgbtq folks & friends in Down East

Maine; July Poetry & NYC Poe Groups; North Fork community; and to the indy, lesbian feminist publishers and small press movements.

Gratitude for time and space to write to Cummington Community of the Arts, MacDowell, Millay Arts, Ucross, Vermont Studio Center, Virginia Center for the Creative Arts and Ann Stokes at Welcome Hill.

Many of the poems from previous books, some in different versions, were published in magazines, journals, anthologies, online publications, exhibited as broadsides and performed in original musical compositions. Thanks to the editors, composers, curators, and organizers who helped bring these poems into the world.

New & Reclaimed Poems, © by Beatrix Gates, 2021-2023:
"A mask for a male goat pretending to be a turnip" appeared in *Afterthought*, Brooksville, ME.
"A mask for a rhinoceros praying to the moon" and "A mask for a stone trying to be discovered" appeared online in *Anthem Journal*.
"How to be carried, March to April" appeared in *Bateau Lit Mag 9.1*, College of the Atlantic, Bar Harbor, Maine.
"Last night" and "Outpost" appeared online in *Cable Street*, Issue 3, Summer 2023.
"Sunspots" appeared in *Dos*, © Beatrix Gates, Finishing Line Press, Georgetown, KY, 2014.
"Songs for Faerie Kingdom" which include "Song for Ron;" "A mask for a male goat pretending to be a turnip;" "A mask for a rhinoceros praying to the moon;" "A mask for a stone trying to be discovered;" "Early Days" and "I Give You Stories" were exhibited for the Farm/Arts Exchange at The Gallery Within, "Collaboration, Poetry & Masks, Beatrix Gates and Ron King," Reversing Falls Sanctuary, Brooksville, Maine, 2014.

native tongue, © by bea gates, 1973, hopalong press, and further poems, 1976:
Thanks to those who supported the poetry & making of a limited edition of *native tongue* from hopalong press: Antioch College; Clifford Burke; Betsy Davids; Eric Horsting; Joan Kleban; Ann Mihalick; Gray Parrot; Bea Sennewald; Twinrocker & the 70's Bay Area Book Arts scene. I received invaluable assistance in building hopalong press, the printshop and small press, in Monterey, Massachusetts from my brother David Gates; Gerard Fulton; Alice Brock; Mrs. Frederic Colby who on her 80th birthday came by to be sure that I had set up a printshop with her equipment; Alice & Joel Schick; Al Silverstein, Jim Youngerman & the New Marlboro crew.

"aside" appeared in *The Second Berkshire Anthology*, eds. Canner and Collins, The Bookstore Press, 1975.
The broadside, "for Gerard," designed and printed by Gates, was exhibited as "Broadsides

& Collages," at the Paddle Wicker Gallery in Lenox Massachusetts, 1976, curated by Bart Arnold and Judy Graham.

The broadside, "Matt's Room: Looking Towards Mount Hunger, Monterey," was designed and printed by Gates for Matt Tannenbaum, proprietor of The Bookstore in Lenox, Massachusetts in 1976 in an edition of 2. The poem appears here in a revised version.

The broadside "window," designed and printed by Gates, was included in the letterpress exhibit organized by lee sharkey for the 1978 Maine Poets Festival at the College of the Atlantic, Bar Harbor, Maine. The poem appears here in a revised version.

Notes on the edition of *native tongue*:

native tongue was designed and printed in a first edition of 138 copies under the hopalong press imprint by press founder Gates. The edition, handset in Deepdene, was printed on a Vandercook proof press at California College of Arts & Crafts in Oakland, California and completed on a Chandler and Price platen press in the Antioch College Engineering Building in Yellow Springs, Ohio in the summer of 1973.

37 copies of the edition were printed letterpress on cotton rag paper with blue jean end papers handmade by Twinrocker. A few copies were bound over boards by Gates with watercolor images on the cover. The remaining copies of the edition were bound by Gates under the supervision of Gray Parrot at his bindery in Hancock, Maine—a few in marble paper with half leather hand-stamped bindings and several copies in buckram over boards. 101 copies were printed on Curtis Rag, perfect bound as trade paperbacks, cover photograph by P. Stewart and lettering for the spine by Joan Kleban.

Shooting at Night, © by Bea Gates, 1980, Granite Press * East, Penobscot, Maine:
Particular gratitude goes to Leslie Chatterton for supporting the poetry, the work at the press, and for finding the perfect location for Granite Press, for years to come, in Penobscot. Big thanks to those friends who helped move equipment and build the printshop in the old canning factory in Penobscot, Maine.

Shooting at Night was published with support from the Maine State Commission for the Arts and Humanities under the directorship of Stuart Kestenbaum.
"Dream Pivot in the Night" appeared in *Blue Unicorn*.
"Mrs. Cratty's Apparition" appeared in *A Spectra I Anthology*, 1979 and in *The Maine Poets Festival Book*, 1979.
"The Balloonist" appeared in *Negative Capability*.

Notes on the edition of *Shooting at Night*:
Shooting at Night was published in a letterpress, limited edition of 150 copies, numbered and signed by the author. Set in Monotype Van Dijk by Michael Bixler, Boston, Massachusetts,

the edition was designed and printed by Gates at Granite Press in Penobscot, Maine. 130 copies of the edition were printed on Ingres Fabriano and bound over boards; 20 copies of the edition were printed on Hosho with handmade Japanese paper overleaf on the title page and bound in Japanese stencil paper over boards by Gray Parrot.

In the Open, © by Beatrix Gates, 1998 Painted Leaf Press, New York City:
Thanks to the late Bill Sullivan, publisher of Painted Leaf Books, for his commitment to lgbtq poetry, and thanks to Jim Wentzy for recording and broadcasting "Triptych" from the living room on W. 12th Street for AIDS Community Television Show, New York City in the early 1990's.

QE2 –Bermuda to New York / Gunbeat by Bea Gates / Meredith Stricker was published first as a letterpress limited edition folio. Designed collaboratively by Gates & Stricker, with an illustration by Stricker, the edition was printed in three colors by Gates, hand-painted, and bound by Gates and Stricker over boards with a Japanese binding, San Francisco, 1980.

"Esprit de Corps" appeared in *Shooting at Night*, Granite Press * East, Penobscot, Maine, 1980.
"Hawk" appeared in *The Long Story*.
"May 14, 1980" appeared as "Variation on a Sestina" in *The Women's Review of Books*.
"Natural Enemies" appeared in *Sinister Wisdom*.
"Negotiations" appeared in *North Dakota Quarterly*.
"Pond," published as "Sonnet #1," appeared in *The Women's Review of Books*.
"Sparks Street" appeared in *Bottomfish*.
"Wild Blue" and "Family Tree" appeared in *Nimrod*.
"Triptych" appeared in *The Kenyon Review (Theatre Issue)* edited by Marilyn Hacker.
Grateful acknowledgment to editors of the anthologies where these poems appeared:
"Deadly Weapon" in *Gay & Lesbian Poetry in Our Time*, eds. Morse and Larkin, Saint Martin's Press.
"Dream: Bay Foal" in *The Key to Everything*, ed. Pearlberg, Saint Martin's Press.
"Conversation with the Body" and "I wrap myself" in *Naming the Waves, Contemporary Lesbian Poetry*, ed. McEwen, Crossing Press and Virago.
"Pond," reprinted as "Sonnet #1," in *My Lover Is A Woman*, ed. Newman, Ballantine Books.
"Refuge, 3." in *The Zenith of Desire*, ed. Pearlberg, Crown.
"Triptych" in *The World in Us: Lesbian & Gay Poetry of the Next Wave*, eds. Lassell and Georgiou, St. Martin's Press.
"Triptych"— "II. Cathy" in *The Arc of Love*, ed., Coss, Scribners.
"Triptych"— "III. Homeless" in *Things Shaped in Passing, More "Poets for Life" Writing from the AIDS Pandemic*, eds. Klein & McCann, Persea Books.

The Poems of Vikram Babu by Jesús Aguado, HOST Publications, Austin, Texas, 2008, translation © 2008 by Electa Arenal / Beatrix Gates. Introduction © 2008 by Beatrix Gates / Electa Arenal. Los Poemas de Vikram Babu, © 2001, Hiperión. Reprinted by permission of the poet.

Many thanks to Jesús Aguado for his inspired poems and for welcoming us in Malaga, Spain where we began the translations. A Witter Bynner Award and residency at The Santa Fe Art Institute offered time to gather Aguado's work and give a first reading of his poetry in translation. Alice Brock provided a window to the sea in Provincetown at the outset of the translations. Thanks to the late Joe Bratcher, publisher of HOST Publications, and Anand Ramaswamy for their commitment to the book; and thanks to POETS HOUSE, Lee Briccetti, Jane Preston, Stephen Motika, and HOST Publications for co-sponsoring the bilingual Reading and Conversation with Jesús Aguado, Electa Arenal and Beatrix Gates about translation, Aguado's work, and Iberian poetry in 2010.

"Like the one who kills then skins a child..." by Jesús Aguado translated by Electa Arenal / Beatrix Gates appeared in *POETS AGAINST THE WAR*, ed. Hamill, The Nation Books, 2003.

A selection of Aguado's poems, translated by Arenal / Gates, appeared in *Sirena: Poesía, arte y cultura* (2006: 2), published by Johns Hopkins University Press.

A selection of Aguado's poems, translated by Arenal / Gates, appeared in *The Dirty Goat*, published by HOST Publications (no. 18, 2008).

Notes on *The Poems of Vikram* and the poet Jesús Aguado:
Jesús Aguado, poet, translator & literary critic. Born in 1961 (Madrid), he has lived in Seville, Malaga, Benares (India) and currently lives in Barcelona. Among his recent books: *El fugitivo*. Poesía reunida: 1984-2010; *La insomne*. Essential Anthology; *Sueños para Ada*; *Carta al padre* and THERIGATA: Poemas budistas de mujeres sabia / Buddhist Poems of Wise Women. He has been honored with Hiperión, Manuel Alcántara and Antonio Oliver Belmas Poetry Awards.

From the *Introduction* by Beatrix Gates / Electa Arenal to *The Poems of Vikram Babu:*
Jesús Aguado is a poet of Andalucía who has laid claim to his own imagination through the invention of distinct voices in his poetry. Aguado has said that to avoid any set identity, form, or ideology, every poetry collection has required a different teller. A sentiment echoed by his fellow *sevillano*, Antonio Machado (1875–1939), when he said that "as a lyric poet my 'I' is never the same." Some of the major figures of Spain's great poetic heritage have been from the southern provinces—Luis de Góngora (Córdoba) in the sixteenth century, and Federico García Lorca (Granada) in the twentieth. Aguado, operating outside the conceptual lyricism of a Góngora or dramatic lyricism of a García Lorca, has turned a different kind of magnifier on the world that has led to more questions than

answers. Aguado adopts the voice of Vikram Babu, a seventeenth-century Indian mystic and basket-weaver who invites us to take part in the work. As poet Jaime Manrique has surmised: "Vikram Babu asks simple questions about profound matters. Or is it profound questions about self-evident truths? Ultimately, Vikram Babu's poems pose the great philosophical questions. Yet the poems themselves are so generous that, for a glorious moment, we feel privy to glimpses of the disquieting beauty, and power, of Truth." Just as Aguado has invented diverse voices, he has been invented by them. *The Poems of Vikram Babu* began as an homage to the tradition of Indian devotional verse, and it was while assembling *Antología de poesía devocional de la India* (Anthology of Devotional Poetry of India) in Benares, that the voice of seventeenth-century Indian basket weaver, Vikram Babu, spoke to Aguado's imagination. The poet quite suddenly found "what I am, what I am not, and what I do not know. Vikram Babu could say things I could not say."

Ten Minutes, © by Beatrix Gates, 2006, Firm Ground Press, Old Lyme, Connecticut; reprint 2011:
Thanks to Victoria Hallerman for supporting this publication.
"Nothing to Hide" appeared in the first issue of *BLOOM, Queer Fiction, Art, Poetry and More* and was included in *The Tulip Anthology* by Ron van Dongen, Hachette.
"To the Editor of the Ellsworth American—1876" was part of the libretto for *The Singing Bridge,* composed by Anna Dembska, Opera House Arts, Stonington, Maine, 2005.
"The Bear" appeared in *TO LOVE, Poems to Commemorate the Occasion of Marie Ponsot's 80th Birthday,* compiled by Alfred Corn and Marilyn Hacker, 2001.
"The Bear," a cantata, composed by Anna Dembska, was performed by the Schoodic Summer Chorus, Schoodic Arts for All, Winter Harbor, Maine, 2003.
"Seeking Tenderness" appeared in *BLOOD & TEARS, A Matthew Shepard Anthology,* edited by Scott Gibson, Painted Leaf Press, 2000, now in print with University of Wisconsin Press.

Dos, © by Beatrix Gates, 2014, Finishing Line Press, Georgetown, KY:
"Conditions" and sections "II. The Knife", "IV. Inside the Wind" and "V." from the long poem, "Dos," appeared in *Sinister Wisdom.*
"Epiphany" appeared in *The Gay & Lesbian Review.*
"Salvia Mexicana" appeared in *The Holly Rose Review.*

desire lines, © by Beatrix Gates, 2020, Artifact Press, Richmond, VA:
desire lines, a letterpress, limited edition of 40 copies, chapbook, Artifact 2020.001.
Thanks to Heidi Reszies, founder of Artifact Books, for the design, printing and illustration, and to Colleen Lawrence for the flax & abaca paper handmade for the edition at the University of Iowa, Center for the Book in Iowa City. Thanks to Mia Kanazawa for her generous conversation.

Uncollected Poems (1984-2023), © by Beatrix Gates, 2023:

"Blueprint" and "The Verge" appeared in *Beloit Poetry Journal*, Vol. 65, No. 2, 2014-2015.

"Burying Winter" and "Dear _____," Finalist for the Tupelo Quarterly Poetry Contest, judged by Alicia Ostriker," appeared in *TQ3*, April 2014.

"Daylight stunned in purpling tongues" and "Determining Charles Homer Haskins" appeared in *The Dirty Goat 20*.

"Dear Half" appeared in *Hummingbird: Magazine of the Short Poem*.

"Fado" appeared in *The Puckerbrush Review*.

"Falling" appeared in *CutBank 23*.

"For Orlando: Make Beautiful in Maine" was published in *Do Not Make the Map Magazine*, Glasgow, Scotland, UK.

"Layover" appeared as "Seattle Layover" online in *Cultural Daily*.

"My mother lately" was published in *The Blue Hill Packet*, Blue Hill, Maine, 2018.

"Neighbor" appeared in *Bateau Lit Mag 9.1*, College of the Atlantic, Bar Harbor, Maine, 2020.

"Oak, November" appeared in *Ploughshares*, Winter 2018-19, Vol. 34., No. 4.

"The Card, the Note, the Envelope" appeared online in *Poetry Northwest, Poetry & Interview* / "*Not Some Side Trip: A Conversation with Beatrix Gates* by Jaimie Li, 2020.

"Then I dreamt about Eva," appeared online in *Cable Street, Issue 3*, Summer 2023.

"Wind's split octaves" was published in *Poetry to Heal Your Blues* compiled by Marilyn Hacker, Portable Poetry, MQ Publications, 2005.

CLOSE APART: Beatrix Gates, poetry, & Tim Seabrook, etchings. Inspired by a selection of poems, spanning 1973-2021, from *native tongue, Shooting at Night, In the Open, Ten Minutes* and *Dos*, printmaker Seabrook created a suite of seven etchings with color by Leslie Cummins featured in Word. Blue Hill Literary Arts Festival at the Cynthia Winings Gallery in Blue Hill, Maine curated by Lee Lehto in 2022. A documentary film, *Close Apart: Beatrix Gates, poetry, & Tim Seabrook, etchings*, made by Matt Shaw was commissioned and supported by the Anahata Foundation about the collaboration during the Pandemic for Word. Blue Hill Literary Arts Festival in 2021. Thanks to Leslie Cummins & Tim Seabrook for the collaboration which led to what became *The Burning Key: New & Selected Poems*. (backlightgrafika.com; www.beatrixgates.org).

The Maine Women Writers Collection at the University of New England houses Beatrix Gates's papers documenting her career as a poet, letterpress printer, designer and publisher of Granite Press and hopalong press. The collection includes letterpress limited editions, Book Arts, production materials and business records.

The Book Arts collection at Bowdoin's Hawthorne Longfellow Library holds copies of letterpress, limited editions from Granite Press, and letterpress printing commissions, designed and printed by Beatrix Gates.

About the Author

Beatrix Gates has published six poetry collections, including *Dos* and Lambda Poetry Award Finalist, *In the Open*. She has been a fellow at MacDowell, Millay Arts, Monson Arts, the Huntington Library, Ucross and VCCA, and she received a Maine Arts Commission Poetry Award. Her hybrid work appears in *Jane Cooper: A Radiance of Attention*. She shared NEA support, as librettist, for *The Singing Bridge* with composer Anna Dembska, and a Witter Bynner Translation Award with Electa Arenal for Jesús Aguado's *The Poems of Vikram Babu*. In 2021, the collaboration, "Close Apart: Beatrix Gates, poetry, & Tim Seabrook, etchings," drawn from Gates' poems from 1973 to 2021, was exhibited at the Cynthia Winnings Gallery for the Word. Blue Hill Literary Arts Festival, and a documentary by Matt Shaw was commissioned on the collaboration with Anahata Foundation support (websites: backlightgrafika.com and www.beatrixgates.org)

Gates founded Granite Press (1976-1989) in Penobscot, Maine, as a Book Artist, job printer and feminist small press publisher. She published Grace Paley's *Leaning Forward*, Joan Larkin's *A Long Sound*, the bilingual *IXOK AMAR.GO, Central American Women Poets for Peace* and letterpress editions by Rosa Lane and Jean Valentine. She has taught writing for 25 years in graduate and undergraduate programs, including City College of New York, Colby College, MFA programs at Goddard and NYU, and in many rural and urban community settings. She holds an MFA from Sarah Lawrence College and BA from Antioch College. She grew up in Cambridge, Massachusetts and has had significant time in NYC and San Francisco. She lives in Maine.